Strategic Prayer

By
Raphael Grant

Strategic Prayer

All scriptures are quoted from the King James Version
of the Bible unless otherwise indicated.

Published by: **To His Glory Publishing Company, Inc.**
463 Dogwood Drive, NW
Lilburn, GA 30047
(770) 458-7947
www.tohisglorypublishing.com

To Contact Raphael Grant:

www.eagleschapel.com

This book is available at:
Amazon.com, BarnesandNoble.com,
Booksamillion.com, etc.
and available in Canada, UK, Australia, etc.

www.tohisglorypublishing.com
(770) 458-7947

ISBN: 978-1-942724-05-6

Dedication

This book is dedicate to Aretha who is my best friend, my lover and my companion. Thank you for allowing me to work on this book in the late hours of the night without complaining. Love you Aretha, you are the best.

This book is also dedicate to Zuriel and Zephan for allowing me to do what God has called me to do. You are my inspiration and because of you, I want to fulfill my God-given mandate. I cherish you guys; you mean the world to me. I love you guys.

Table of Contents

Acknowledgements

Thank you "Papa" Archbishop Nicholas Duncan-Williams for being a father to me. I appreciate your mentorship and the enormous impact you made on my life and my ministry. We stand on your shoulders to do exploits all over the world.

I say a big "thank you" to the entire Family of Eagle's Chapel International Ministry (Prayer City). You are precious and such an amazing family of which anyone would want to be a part; you are the envy of every Pastor. Love you Guys.

Preface

In the Pentecostal Charismatic churches today, lots of prayers go on but with little results. One of the reasons for this is that the prayers are not born out of revelation. In order for our prayers to be potent and affective, we must pray with the understanding of what we are dealing with or what we are up against; otherwise it is a waste of time and energy.

Therefore, in this season of great harvest and great attacks from the kingdom of darkness, our prayers must be strategic and effective. I have had so many people come up to me saying, "I have prayed all the prayers but I am not getting any results or answers." It is reason why the Lord told me to write this book and to teach the Church how to pray strategic prayers to get results.

Jesus' Name is the most powerful and ultimate weapon there is; the ultimate strategy of the Church. In the power and authority of His name, we have everything we need to drive the forces of satan out of our homes, our cities and the nations. Jesus' Name is All-powerful, Indestructible and Unchangeable! It legitimately belongs to us. However, we must reach out by faith to take it and use it in our own circumstances or its power will never be realized in our lives. Until the Church rises up with the full revelation of the power that is in Jesus' Name, we will not be able to operate in the power that God intended.

Jesus has given us His Power of Attorney! What this means is that we have the legal authority to use His name to take authority over satan and exercise domino on the earth. Before He ascended into the heavens, He told the disciples, "All power is given unto me in heaven and in earth" (Matthew

28:18). He then delegated the power and authority to His Church –to you and me! We are to rule in heaven and on earth. As we see in the scripture below, the Lord Jesus compared Himself to a man who is going on a long journey and left his servants in charge of his house:

> **"For the Son of man is as a man taking a far journey, who left his house, and gave authority to his servants, and to every man his work, and commanded the porter to watch"** (Mark 13:34).

This is exactly what He has done. Jesus finished the work that He was given by the Father. He destroyed the works of the devil. Through His obedience unto death, He defeated satan and stripped him of his power over us. As a result, He was exalted, given the name that is above all names and before ascending into heaven, He gave the Church the legal right to use His Name. He restored dominion of the earth back to us and gave us His name with the power and authority to exercise His dominion over the earth.

The earth does not belong to satan, it belongs to the Son of the Living God! The Lord Jesus intended for His Church to reign with Him by the power invested in His Name. Jesus did not intend for the Church to be powerless and defeated. The Apostle Paul told the believers in Rome that, "For if by the transgression of the one, death reigned through the one, much more those who receive the abundance of grace and of the gift of righteousness will reign in life through the One, Jesus Christ (Romans 5:17 NAS).

Note that Paul said, "Much more." I like these words because satan sent sin, sickness, and death to reign on this earth through Adam's sin in the Garden of Eden but praise God, Jesus "dethroned" satan. Now, "much more," not less but "much more," we reign in this life through Jesus Christ! We are not "second class citizens" but we are kings and priests unto God. Not only has Christ promised that those who overcome will one day rule and reign on earth with Him for a thousand years, but today, we can rule and reign with the power and authority of His Name. Think about Christ sitting on the throne, possessing All-power, All-authority and All-dominion in heaven, on earth and in hell. He is on His throne and spiritually, you are sitting on the throne with Him. Physically, you are on this earth but you possess that same power and authority in His Name. Therefore, you can root out satan and reign in this earth together with the Lord.

We are not waiting to be delivered out of satan's hands; we are already delivered! We are not waiting to become heirs of God and joint heirs with Jesus, we are heirs and joint heirs now –Ephesians 1:10-11:

> **"That in the dispensation of the fulness of times he might gather together in one all things in Christ, both which are in heaven, and which are on earth; even in him: 11 In whom also we have obtained an inheritance, being predestinated according to the purpose of him who worketh all things after the counsel of his own will."**

We are not waiting to be seated with Christ in heavenly places, we are seated with Him now! The same resurrection power that raised Christ from the dead has made us alive. It has translated us out of satan's dominion and raised us up together with Christ where He is now seated — Ephesians 1:21:

> **"Far above all principality, and power, and might, and dominion, and every name that is named, not only in this world, but also in that which is to come."**

This is our legitimate position today! Knowing this, we can pray strategically and also effectively because victory is already assured! Praise God!

Introduction

God is raising a people for Himself: A people who will rise up to stand in the gap and possess the gates of His enemies. He said:

> **"Ask of me, and I shall give thee the heathen for thine inheritance, and the uttermost parts of the earth for thy possession. Thou shalt break them with a rod of iron; thou shalt dash them in pieces like a potter's vessel"** (Psalm 2:8-9).

As the children of Zion, God wants us to pray and ask Him for the heathen as our inheritance and the uttermost parts of the earth for our possession. It will take a great battle and travailing of the soul in another realm of prayer to accomplish this. This "end time harvest" is a militant harvest. To be able to antagonize and halt the devil's agenda, will take much spiritual warfare and agonizing in prayer on another level and frequency to bring divine infusion of divine capacity. The Prophet Isaiah says:

> **"For Zion's sake will I not hold my peace, and for Jerusalem's sake I will not rest, until the righteousness thereof go forth as brightness, and the salvation thereof as a lamp that burneth"** (Isaiah 62:1).

God is raising a generation who will not hold its peace or rest until it sees the souls that had been snatched into hell by the devil being harvested into the Kingdom of our Lord Jesus Christ. For the Bible says in Jeremiah:

> **"Behold, I am the LORD, the God of all flesh: is there any thing too hard for Me?"** (Jeremiah 32:27).

If we, as children of God, rise up and bombard the kingdom of hell and its manipulative acts through prayer, will there be "any thing too hard" for the Lord?

> **"Am I a God at hand, saith the LORD, and not a God afar off?"** (Jeremiah 23:23).

Our God is not a God who is afar off. He is nearer than we can ever think or imagine. By "invoking and activating" through prayers, we can apprehend the strategies of the devil. Jeremiah says:

> **"The fierce anger of the LORD shall not return, until he have done it, and until he have performed the intents of his heart: in the latter days ye shall consider it"** (Jeremiah 30:24).

God is raising a people who prays and gets results for, without a praying people, there will be no results.

Beloved, you think you are praying, but I have come to inform you that there are levels of prayers, and there is a level of prayer that is unstoppable and cannot be hindered. It will take you knowing the Word of God, and being informed, to come to that level and realm of capacity. The scripture admonishes us as follows:

> **"Be wise now therefore, O ye kings: be instructed, ye judges of the earth"** (Psalms 2:10).

It will require you instructing, and not suggesting, to overrule the kingdoms of darkness, and that is exactly what this book intends to expose to you: The instructions you need to be able to stir up the LORD to arise and defend your cause and to execute judgment over principalities, powers, thrones, dominions, authorities, insights, and to dislodge the covert operations of the satanic hosts and agents of hell.

> **"And having spoiled principalities and powers, he made a show of them openly, triumphing over them in it"** (Colossians 2:15).

> **"For by him were all things created, that are in heaven, and that are in earth, visible and invisible, whether they be thrones, or dominions, or principalities, or powers: all things were created by him, and for him: And he is before all things, and by him all things consist"** (Colossians 1:16-17).

In the name of Jesus, things in heaven, things on earth, and things under the earth must bow because He is the risen Lord. God bless you as you read on.

Chapter 1
Put the Devil Where He Belongs

The Womb as the Entrance to Humanity

For human beings, the **only legal entry point into the earth** is through the womb of a women. This is the divine as well as the natural law and anything outside of this is illegal. **Therefore, when God wanted to redeem humanity and reconcile man back to Himself, even He had to come through the womb of a woman!** This is why the Savior was born of a virgin; a woman!

Satan is an Illegal Occupant

Satan is here on earth illegally because **he did not come through the womb of a women** –the legal entering point! He **fell from heaven** to earth. In **Luke 10:18,** the Lord said to His disciples, **"I beheld satan as lightning <u>fall</u> from heaven."** Also in **Revelation 12:7-12** it is written:

"And there was war in heaven: Michael and his angels fought against the dragon; and the dragon fought and his angels, 8 And prevailed not; neither was their place found any more in heaven. 9 And the great dragon was cast out, that old serpent, called the Devil, and satan, which deceiveth the whole world: he was cast out into the earth, and his angels were cast out with him. 10 And I heard a loud voice saying in heaven, Now is come salvation, and strength, and the kingdom of our God, and the power of his Christ: for the accuser of our brethren is cast down, which accused them before our God day and night… 12 Therefore rejoice, ye heavens, and ye that dwell in them. **Woe to the inhabiters of the earth and of the sea! for the devil is come down unto you, having great wrath, because he knoweth that he hath but a short time."**

Satan has been defeated and stripped of his power over us by the Lord Jesus Christ. As a result, satan has been operating illegally here on the earth. We have been given **power** "over all power of the enemy" (Luke 10:19). Yet, because we have failed to exercise the authority that belongs to us in Jesus' Name, satan has continued to attack us with every form of sickness and disease. He has continued to attack our homes and loved ones. Look around you and you will see how we have allowed the devil to take too much territory. We cannot continue to sit back and allow satan to gain control of our government through ungodly leaders. We cannot allow him to gain control of our school systems. We cannot allow him to fill out cities with every form of sin, crime, pornography and destroy people's lives through drugs and alcohol addiction.

As you listen to newscast on television or read the newspaper concerning conditions of the world today, you notice that they are filled with news of violence, addictions, struggles for freedom and liberty, growing immorality, sexual perversions, growing problems with commissions, etc. **It would seem as if satan still holds dominion over this earth but the truth is that it is the Church that has dominion.** It is the Church's responsibility to root out satan.

God is not going to do it because He has chosen to work through His Church — through you and me! It is up to us to cast out the devil to where he belongs. In other words, cast him to his side of the line. Like a mighty army, we shall go forward into battle in the power and authority of Jesus' Name and drive satan out and take dominion of the earth. It is time we rise up and exercise our sovereign authority over the devil and his diabolical activities. He cannot go any further than he already has because you have the power, so use it efficiently in stopping the devil in his tracks.

Your Divine Authority

During the last weeks of Jesus' life, before his mediatorial death and resurrection, He gave His disciples some special instructions concerning prayer. These were among His deepest teachings. **One of His primary emphases was that His disciples were to bring their petitions to God in His Name. No leader has ever given such amazing authority in the advancement of his kingdom.** Therefore, we need to answer three questions concerning His Name: What does the name imply in Jewish thoughts? What does it mean to pray in Jesus' Name? How can we use Jesus' Name more effectively in our prayers?

Chapter 2
The Meaning of Jesus' Name in Jewish Thoughts

The Name as it was used in the time of Christ implied three things. The Name is the person and to praise the Name of Jesus is to praise Jesus Himself. To love the Name of Jesus is to love Jesus. To dishonor the Name of Jesus is to insult Jesus because your name is your person. The name of a person represents all we know of the person.

When Moses hungered to draw closer to Jehovah, he asked to see His glory. God replied that a regular human being (meaning a person not born again) could not survive such a divine encounter because His glory would be greater than the physical body could bear but God promised to reveal Himself partially to Moses. He put Moses in the cleft of a rock, covered him with His hand and passed in front of Moses. He removed His hand for a second so that Moses could see His back side after He had passed by. **As He passed by, He proclaimed His Name** as we see in the following scriptures in **Exodus 34:6-7:**

> **"And the LORD passed by before him, and proclaimed, The LORD, The LORD God, merciful and gracious, longsuffering, and abundant in goodness and truth, 7 Keeping mercy for thousands, forgiving iniquity and transgression and sin, and that will by no means clear the guilty; visiting the iniquity of the fathers upon the children, and upon the children's children, unto the third and to the fourth generation."**

God forgives wickedness, rebellion and sin but He does not leave the guilty unpunished. **To know God is to know all that His Name represents and to understand that Name is**

to see God. Also, the Name of Jesus represents all that we know of Him from scripture and from personal experience. It includes His transforming power, His love, His mercy, His intolerance of hypocrisy and His desire for us to be holy as He is holy. It includes our knowledge of Him in His external glory, His creation of the universe, His incarnation, His atoning death, His pressurization and His coming back again. The name is the person of Jesus actively present to the early Christians; they were all gathered "in the Name of Jesus."

> **"And whatsoever ye do in word or deed, do all in the Name of the Lord Jesus**, giving thanks to God and the father by him"** (Colossian 3:17).

This means acting by the authority of Jesus and manifesting His character. When we act in Jesus Name today, we likewise believe that we are not acting alone but with Jesus by our side even though He is invisible to our eyes.

What it Means to Pray in Jesus' Name

Several important concepts must be kept in mind before you can pray in Jesus' Name. **Praying in Jesus' Name is only possible if you are "In Jesus."** Jesus said:

> **"I will do whatever you ask in my name, so that the Son may bring Glory to the Father. You may ask for anything in my name and I will do it"** (John 14:13-14).

In the same conversation with his disciples and shortly before his death, He said to them:

> **"If ye abide in me, and my words abide in you, ye shall ask what ye will, and it shall be done unto you"** (John 15:7).

Jesus used the phases **'In Me'** several times in John 14 and 15 to mean, **"In Jesus Name."**

1. To be in spiritual unity with Jesus (John 15: 4-7)

2. To be in the Vine (John 15:4)

3. To be in Jesus' Love (John 15: 9-10)

In John 13 through 16, we are told that love must be mutual and if it is to be received, it must be responded to. His new command is love. You cannot love Jesus unless you love His other children. To love Jesus is to obey Jesus as we see in **John 14:15-23** below:

> **"If ye love me, keep my commandments... Jesus answered and said unto him, If a man love me, he will keep my words: and my Father will love him, and we will come unto him, and make our abode with him."**

If you love Jesus, you will remain in Jesus. To have Jesus living within you is to be indwelled by the Holy Spirit; to have Christ's words remaining in you. Our ability to pray in Jesus' Name depends upon this **"In Christ"** relationship. To pray in Jesus' Name is to be conformed to His nature. The example given in John 13 of Jesus's Name is His servant role of washing the disciples' feet. As you know the truth, you must do the truth as Jesus said in **John 13:17:**

> **"If ye know these thing, happy are ye if ye do them."**

When you joyfully do His will and are reflecting His Christ-likeness, you may pray in Jesus' Name. To Pray in Jesus' Name is to pray for His sake. **You must desire what Jesus said that you request in the spirit of the Lord's Prayer, "Your will be done"** (Matthew 6:10). This was Jesus' attitude as He prayed in the Garden of Gethsemane. You are to pray actively, aggressively that Jesus' will may prevail. To pray in His Name is to insist that His total victory be made manifest in the world. To pray in Jesus' Name is to claim Calvary's victory over your needs because Jesus openly defeated satan and all his evil host of demons.

"And having spoiled principalities and powers, he made a shew of them openly, triumphing over them in it" (Colossians 2:15).

Satan is a defeated foe and a user who tries to frighten and bluff you but he has already lost the last battle. In Jesus' Name, you claim the actualization of the victory Christ won on the Cross.

To pray in Jesus' Name is to acknowledge His full role as God's anointed -your Prophet, Priest and King. As Prophet, He is your Counselor and Guide and as Priest, He is your Intercessor so that as you pray, He adds the "Amen" to your prayer. **Revelation 3:14** reveals to us that Jesus' Name is **Amen**:

"And unto the angel of the church of the Laodiceans write; These things saith the Amen, the faithful and true witness, the beginning of the creation of God."

For all the promises that God made are **"Yes"** in Christ and also through Him they are **"Amen"** to the Glory of God (2 Corinthians 1:20). As King, He is your Sovereign Lord. Therefore, when you pray in His Name, you claim His Prophetic guidance, His Priestly intercession, and His Kingly answer to your prayers.

To pray in Jesus' Name is to pray in all of His authority. He has delegated to you the authority to pray and ask God to accomplish great things in His Name. You can rebuke satan and his schemes, his demons and all his infernal works in the Name of Jesus. This is your protection, your might and your victory. You see, the Lord is not a respecter of persons; He can choose to use anybody in spite of race, ethnicity, culture, gender and background. In fact, credentials and university degrees do not come into play when God decides to use a person **but He is a respecter of His principles. One of those principles is that you cannot go to the Father without passing through Jesus and you cannot receive anything from the Father without using the Name of Jesus.** The reason as we have seen is because the Name of Jesus is what gives you access to the Father.

Getting Your Prayers to the Throne of God

The Lord Jesus is our **Mediator**, **Intercessor**, **Advocate**, and our **Lord**. As such, He stands between us and the Father. **No place in the Bible is it recorded that Jesus told His disciples to pray to Him. Rather, they were always to pray to the Father in Jesus' Name.** If we wish to be sure of reaching the Throne of God with our prayers, we must come to God according to the rules laid down in His Word.

> **"And in that day ye shall ask me nothing. Verily, verily, I say unto you, Whatsoever ye shall ask the Father in my name, he will give it you"** (John 16:23).

Notice that Jesus said **in that day**, ye shall asking me anything. Jesus said this just before He died and rose again to sit at the right hand of the Father on our behalf. This is why He said, "Whatsoever ye shall ask the FATHER IN MY NAME, He will give it to you." Jesus was talking about His **mediatorial position at the right land of the Father** where He would soon ascend and be seated (Hebrew 1:3). Another translation reads, **"In the day you shall <u>not</u> pray to me."** Jesus said, we are to ask the Father in His Name. There is no other way to approach God.

Certainly, we can worship Jesus though worship is a type of prayer. We can tell Jesus how much we love and appreciate Him but when it comes to praying and asking for petitions, we must ask the Father in the Name of the Lord Jesus Christ.

"For this cause I bow my knees unto the Father of our Lord Jesus Christ, 15 Of whom the whole family in heaven and earth is named" (Ephesians 3:14-15).

We are to bow our knees to our Heavenly Father in prayer using the Name of Jesus. It is not as important which church you belong to as it is which family you belong to. Praise the Lord that believers are in the 'Family of God' and that we can approach Father God in prayer in the Name of Jesus! Many people know about praying to God but they do not know anything about praying to the Father in Jesus' Name. In others words, when they are praying, they do not sound as if they really know God as Father through Jesus. He is God to the World but He is Father to us in Christ Jesus. There is a joy knowing that the Father will answer our prayers.

Chapter 3
The Power of Authority

A 'Power of Authority' is also known as **'Power of Attorney.'** It is a legal document authorizing one to act as the attorney or agent of the grantor. A power of Attorney legally appoints an individual to act in another's name and place. **It gives the individuals who has been appointed full power and authority over the personal property and interests belonging to the one granting the Power of Authority. It authorizes the individual named to act on another's person's behalf as they might or could do if they were personally present.**

A Power of Authority gives an individual the power and authority to take whatever action is required or necessary in maintaining all the personal property and interest of the one granting the Power of Authority. **They are given the Power of Authority to determine (at their discretion) the manner in which they will exercise the power which has been delegated to them. A Power of Authority gives the authorized person the power to transact business of any kind in another person's place and on their behalf.** They have the authority to sell, lease and exchange any and all of the grantor's property and valuables. He can borrow money or loan money in grantor's name.

For instance, if you decide to relocate to another state for a long period of time leaving behind your house, your valuables, your car, your furniture, a saving accounts, trust funds, etc., you might decide to name a trusted friend or relative as your legal representative and given them a Power of Authority to act on your behalf while you are gone. During your absence, the person would legally have the power, authority and legal possession of all that you owned and would be able to do whatever they determined best with your property. With the Power of Authority, they would be able to sell all your furnishing and lease your house. They would legally be able to draw upon your saving account, revoke a trust and transfer the money into their own account. They would be able to sell your car and invest the money in stocks and bonds. They would even be to borrow money in your name.

Jesus has ascended into heaven and has given the Church (you and I) the Power of Authority:

- We have been appointed as Christ's legal representatives on this earth and have the legal power and authority to use His Name.

- In Jesus' Name, we have been given full power and authority; including legal access to all that He possess!

- In Jesus' Name, we have been given full power and authority to act on his behalf in the same manner He would act if He were living and walking on this earth.

- In Jesus' Name, we legally possess the same power and authority over all things in heaven, on earth and in hell.

In the natural world, a 'Power of Attorney' is written naming the person who is appointed as an attorney or representative. It lists the extent of the power given to the attorney or representative and it gives full power and authority to act on the grantor's behalf. It is dated, signed by the grantor, notarized, sealed and mailed to the County Recorder's Office to be recorded. **The infallible, impregnable Word of God is your Power of Attorney.** It is a legally binding document authorizing you to act on Christ's behalf with His power and authority. Christ has invested you with what legally belongs to you and has given you instructions on how to carry out His will on this earth. It is legally binding and will stand up in any court.

Christ's Power of Attorney became effective on the **Resurrection morning** in 30 A.D. **It was signed by the Name that is above every name and sealed with the blood of Jesus!** It is legally binding because Almighty God, the Great "I AM", the Creator, the Alpha and Omega and all the host of heaven are backing it up.

Power of Attorney over Forces of Darkness
Through your Power of Authority, you have the legal right in Jesus' Name to take authority over the work of the enemy. **You have been given power over all the power of the enemy (Luke 10:19). In the Name of Jesus, every demon in hell must obey!** We know that today, our struggle is not with flesh and blood. Our battles are not with the members of our families, relatives, friends or co-workers. Almost every day of our lives, we battle against principalities, against powers, against the rulers of darkness of the world and against spiritual wickedness in high places (Ephesians 6:12).

Satan attacks us through our circumstances. He tries to put sickness and disease on our bodies and he places temptations before us. There are oppressing and tormenting spirits released against us such as fear, depression and anxiety. There are addictive spirits that try to bring us into bondage through habits such as pornography, alcohol, nicotine or drugs. They are materialistic and selfish spirits that try to keep your mind occupied on the pleasures and the cares of this life.

Satan has no power or authority to rule over you. Jesus has delivered you out of his dominion. He has "stripped" satan of his power over you. By using the Name of Jesus, you can come against all the power of the enemy and you take dominion over satan and all the evil spirits attacking you. If there are habits in your life that are keeping you in bondage, you need to exercise your legal authority in the Name of Jesus to bind the addictive spirits that are attacking you. If a spirit of fear tries to bind you, the moment you realize what is happening, take authority over it. In Jesus' Name, command it to leave. It must obey the Name of Jesus. When spirits of doubt and confusion come against you, command them to go in the Name of Jesus!

If you have unsaved loved ones who are bound by demons of alcohol, marijuana, cocaine or any other drugs, go into battle using the All-powerful Name of Jesus and command the spirits to lose their hold. Do not continue to plead or beg God to deliver your loved ones out of satan's hands. Jesus Christ has already freed man from satan's dominion. The war has been won and you have been given the Power of Attorney; the full power and authority to act on Christ's behalf and in His name.

Jesus has given you His Name and has told you, "Go!" Therefore, go in His Name and deliver your loved ones out of the hand of the enemy. No matter how insignificant and inadequate you may feel, remember that you are not going on the basis of your own spiritual strength or on the basis of your own righteousness. You are going in the Name that is above every name and you will not be defeated because the great, "I AM" is with you and will give you the victory.

Jesus gave us the right and the authority to use His Name in prayer. He said, **"In my name shall they cast out demons"** that bind men's souls with darkness and disease. I like Kenneth E. Hagin's illustration of this point by using the example of opening a car door. According to him, when you go to your car with a key that unlocks the door, you insert and turn the key. Then you say that you unlock the door but you really did not unlock the door, the key did it. You also have a key that fits the ignition. Ordinarily, you could not start the car without the key. Again, you do not actually start the car, the key does it. They key is the important factor that enables you to unlock and start your car.

I began to look at the authority in the Name of Jesus from the same viewpoint. **In other words, I am not the one who is going to cast out any devils. In the natural, I do not have any authority in myself but Jesus gave me they key to all the authority that I will ever need and it is in His Name. Jesus' Name is the key! His name is the authority!** All I have to do is use the key and the key does the work. This alleviated the fear that I had about my own abilities and authority. I was able to use the Name because the Name is the key and the Name works!

Binding the Works of the Devil in the Name of Jesus

In the first place, I began to see that the devil is the author of all that is evil and wrong. The New Testament says that satan is the God of this world and that he has blinded man from seeing the glorious light of the world:

> **"In whom the god of this world hath blinded the minds of them which believe not**, lest the light of the glorious gospel of Christ, who is the image of God, should shine unto them" (2 Corinthians 4:4).

Several scriptures talk about how the devil tries to bind men's souls. I began to see how members of my own family that are unsaved were bound by the devil and do not understand where they are heading. They were spiritually blinded by the god of this world; satan. For example, no man in his right mind would drive his car on the highway at 100 miles an hour while running the red lights and passing signs that read, 'Danger Ahead' with disregard but a man who is on drugs or drunk will do it because he does not know what he is doing.

No intelligent person in his right mind will go through life wheeling and dealing in sin and purposely plunge off into eternity and into hell. If he does not want to accept Jesus Christ, he is not in his right mind. He is spiritually blind and we see this outlined in the Bible and in the story about the prodigal son. **"When he came to himself, he returned home"** (Luke 15:17). So, there was a time when the prodigal son was not in his right mind but when he came to himself, he decided to go back home.

Secondly, I began to see that the authority that believers possess in the Name of Jesus is in the knowledge that all the power of heaven is at our disposal in that Name. However, if we as believers do not exercise the right and authority, then nothing will be done about our situation. **We must learn how to get bold in the Word of God and how to exercise the power and authority in God's Word that makes prayer work.** To expect prayer to do the job is the same as to expect your physical hand to unlock the car door. In prayer, you need to have faith in the Name of Jesus and in the Word of God in order to get the job done. Again, the Name of Jesus is our key. Sometimes, we think we can move God with our tears, prayers and fasting but God does not ever change. He is always the same.

> "For **I am the Lord, I change not**, therefore you are not consumed o Sons of Jacob" (Malachi 3:6).

It is also written in **Hebrews 13:8:**

> **"Jesus Christ is the same yesterday, today and forever."**

God moves when you come to Him according to His Word. Therefore use the Word and the Name of Jesus as the key to move God's heart. When you do this, then prayer will work for you and you will have your answer. All those years of hindrances, affliction, lack and pain can be overcome through the authority in the Name of Jesus. The Name of Jesus breaks any power, any yoke of the devil and it brings deliverance — that is what settles it.

Let Faith Saturate Your Prayers

The Name of Jesus belongs to you; that Name has authority and power on earth. **As a believer, you have the right to use the Name just as much as I do. However, if the devil can hold you in the thought arena; the area of reasoning, he will whip you. But if you can stay in the arena of Faith, then he is defeated.** We are commanded in **1 Timothy 6: 12** to:

> **"Fight the good fight of faith."**

And also in **1 Peter 5:8-9** we told to:

> **"Be alert and of sober mind. Your enemy the devil prowls around like a roaring lion looking for someone to devour. *9* <u>Resist him, standing firm in the faith</u>, because you know that the family of believers throughout the world is undergoing the same kind of sufferings."**

Another translation says, "Whom resist steadfast in your Faith." **You are to resist the adversary with your faith.** You have to believe in your own heart and with your own spirit that what the Word of God says about Jesus is true and that what the Word says about the devil is true. You have authority over him in the Name of Jesus but the devil will try to fight you. **When I broke his power over my family and our destiny using the Name of Jesus, the devil tried my faith. He tried to get me in the thought realm. Satan tried to pull me in the arena of thought and reasoning.** He tried to get me to think that my destiny and that of my family will not be fulfilled. **This is how many people try to solve their problems with their minds and then they get all confused.** They are practically worried to death; they continually fret and are anxious.

Your heart is your spirit; you believe God's Word with your spirit which is inside of you. Then, shut your mind off to doubt, unbelief and thoughts that are contrary to the Word of God. You must believe in your heart and act from the inside of your heart. Jesus said, **"Whosever shall say and shall not doubt in his heart"** (Mark 11:23). This is the principle that is involved in believing God and receiving answers to prayers.

"For I say, through the grace given into me, to every man that is among you, not to think of yourself more highly than he ought to thin, but to think soberly, **according as God's dealt to every man the measure of Faith"** (Romans 12:3).

God has dealt to every man the measure of faith. Therefore, every believer can receive answers to his or her prayers. If you say you do not have faith, then you are making God out to be a liar. **You do have faith; everyman has faith. It is the thinking**

faith and speaking faith (words) that lead the heart out of defeat into victory. In other words, you need to use the faith you have in order for it to be effectual.

Do not accept no for an answer and do not be denied! In Christ Jesus and as a recreated blood bought child of God, it is your 'family right', your redemptive right, your Gospel right, your God-given right to have what God has promised you. Therefore, appropriate by faith what belongs to you and it will come. It is your 'now' faith, so accept God's Word. Believe it and it will become a reality in your life.

Chapter 4
Strategic Prayers

To get the results of answered prayers, the prayer must be strategic. **Prayer has a long arm and it can reach all the way to Heaven.** The Scripture teaches this truth through beautiful symbolisms such as the raising of the hands "In prayer:"

"Let us lift up our hearts and our hands to God in Heaven" (Lamentation 3: 41).

Not only can your prayers reach heaven, but the arm of prayer can also span the miles to any part of the world. In your place of intercession, you can also touch someone who needs you thousands of miles away. This is not make-believe; this is spiritual reality.

Strategic prayers can give you instant entrance into any home, hospital, government office and the courtroom in any part of the world. Just as distance cannot hinder your reach or touch through prayer, neither walls nor "No Entry" signs can halt your presence or stay your hand off a surgeon as he operates on a friend or a loved one. Through prayer, your unseen presence can be with the loved one through the operation.

As revealed in the New Testament, Paul the Apostle of strategic prayers, prayed constantly for his coverts and the churches he founded in many places. Indeed, his prayer was so real and earnest that he actually believed that though he was physically separated from them, his spirit was with them as he prayed. It is in fact what Paul was talking about when he wrote to the church in Corinth:

"When you are assembled in the name of Lord Jesus and I am with you in spirit and the power of the Lord Jesus is present" (1 Corinthians 5:4).

As we can see from the above scripture, Paul did not hesitate to tell these very saints that through prayer, he would meet with them as they handled a case of church discipline. **Paul was maintaining spiritual contact through strategic prayer.** Again, Paul wrote similar words to the saints in the Colossians church.

"Though I am absent from you in body, I am present with you in spirit and delight to see how orderly you are and how firm your faith in Christ is" (Colossians 2:5).

The church lived so vividly in Paul's prayer that it was as if he was right there with them. **Paul identified with Colossians through strategic prayers, fasting and intercession that he knew it was a spiritual fact that he could be with them through prayer.** This depth of identification in prayer is not common today but it is a glorious possibility if we walk closely with God. Through strategic prayer, you can place your guiding hand on the steering wheel of a car, enter into the hall of justice and place your affirming hand on the shoulder of the Judge. **Through strategic prayer you can place your restraining hand on the arm of a criminal or terrorist anywhere in the world.**

In the Old Testament, the book of Exodus shows us a first-hand account of the use of a **strategic hand** in the battle between the children of Israel and the Amalekites. **Moses instructed Joshua to lead God's people into battle while he (Moses) lifted up his hands and as long as his hands were up, Israel was winning.** When Moses's hands grew tired and he lowered them, the Amalekites began to win. **Therefore, they placed a stone under Moses for him to sit on while Aaron and Hur held**

up his hands on each side so that his hands would remained steady till sunlight. As a result, Joshua overcame the Amalekite army with the sword. Then the Lord said to Moses, "Write this on a scroll as something to be remembered" (Exodus 17: 11-14). What is the explanation of this great victory and why should it be remembered? Moses gave us the answer in verse 16, **"Hands were lifted up to the Throne of the Lord."**

When our hands are visibly lifted up, spiritually they touch the throne of God and as a result, you can pray prayers that touch the throne of God. The opposite of this is praying prayers that go no higher than your head and never go beyond your room. When you pray the will of God by the Holy Spirit and in Jesus' Name, your prayers can reach all the way to Heaven! Paul exhorts us in 1 Timothy 2:8, **"I want men everywhere to lift up holy hands in prayer."** Does this mean that we must literally hold up our hands whenever we pray? Most certainly not. God is more concerned that we lift up our hearts and our souls to Him, "To you, Oh Lord I lift up my Soul" (Psalms 25:1, 86:4, 143:8).

Whether we raise our hands literally or not, the essence of prayer is that we lift up our spiritual eyes and hearts to God. During times of earnest intercession or intense spiritual warfare, we may in the privacy of our prayer place or even in public (almost without realizing it), lift our physical hands toward God. **"Hear My Cry for mercy as I call to you for help, as I lift up my hands towards your Most Holy Place"** (Psalms 28:2).

God has given you two weapons through strategic prayer that are more powerful than any other weapon available today. Unlike man-made weapons that are subject to failure, these weapons have been fashioned by Almighty God and are one hundred percent accurate in one hundred percent of the time!

These two powerful weapons will enable you to prepare yourself for battle and to position yourself for victory. They will place you in a position of knowing how to locate the enemy lines, to penetrate it and to tear down strongholds!

These weapons are a vital part of your equipment as a soldier. With these two weapons, you are fully prepared to face your circumstances and the attacks of the enemy. Without these two weapons, you are like a soldier going out to battle with a blindfold over his eyes. You will not be able to detect or locate the enemy, you will not be able to defend yourself, you will not be able to use your other weapons effectively and you will not be able to survive.

God has given you the same powerful weapons that Jesus used to defeat satan. He has commanded you to, use **His Word** and to **"Put on the Full Amour of God"** (Ephesian 6:11). He has given you everything you need to be the strong invincible spiritual warrior that He intended for you to be but you must pick up the weapons and use them. It is not enough for you to be aware that you have these powerful weapons available to you. You may have already known about the weapons of spiritual warfare and you may have even used them in spiritual warfare from time to time but you do not know how to use them in the battles that you currently face in your own life, in your home, on your job or in your ministry.

We know that, "The weapons of our warfare are not carnal, but mighty through God to the pulling down of strong holds" (2 Corinthians 10:4) but, before we can become a powerful and experienced spiritual warrior like Jesus, **we must learn how to activate them**. For example, all the powerful weapons in the United States' arsenal are useless and are totally ineffective until they are activated. A high powered machine gun is powerless until a soldier picks it up, points it at the enemy and pulls the trigger. **As powerful as the spiritual weapons that God has designated and made available for you to use are, they will not be effective in your life until you pick them up, point them at the enemy and pull the trigger.**

Taking Hold of the World through Prayer

There is a powerful living force within you which is the Word of God that makes you invincible through prayer. God has planted something within you that is so strong, so steadfast and sure, it is absolutely incapable of error and cannot be taken by assault. **There is no evil work, no evil power of the enemy that can defeat you; you cannot be taken.** It **is the only thing powerful enough to break satan's hold and enable you to walk in one hundred percent victory.** That powerful force is the unchangeable, infallible, impregnable **Word of God.** Before this powerful strategy that Jesus used against satan; speaking the **Word,** can become reality in your life. You must know what the **Word of God** is.

Take your Bible and hold it in your hand, open it up and read through its pages. **The book that you hold in your hand is God's Word and God's Voice to us; it is sacred and holy.** Every Word in the Bible from cover to cover is divinely inspired. A solemn warning is given to those who would add or take away from the words that are written in it (Revelation 22:18-19). Every prophecy and every Word in it will come to pass. The Bible is the written Word of God but it does not contain every Word that God has ever spoken nor all the things Jesus said and did while He was upon the earth. If it did, there would not be enough books in the world to contain them all.

"And there are also many other things which Jesus did, the which, if they should be written every one, I suppose that even the world itself could not contain the books that should be written. Amen" (John 21:25).

Chapter 5
The Power of the Spoken and Written Word of God

Again, the Bible is God's voice to us but do not limit your understanding to think that it is the sum total of the Word of God. **God's Word is not only the written Word; the Bible, but it is God Himself as the 'The Living Word.' The written Word and the Living Word are inseparable!** The early Church did not have the written Bible as we have today but they spoke the Word of the things they saw and heard concerning Jesus and "the Word of God increased" (Acts 6:7). **They were able to speak the Word with power because the Word was in them.**

There are two Greek Words in the Bible which will help you understand concept more fully: the "Logos" and the "Rehma" Words.

1. "Logos"
The Word **"Logos"** as used in the New Testament has two meanings:

A) **It is an expression of God's thoughts through statements made by God Himself or by Christ.** A man's word is the means that he uses to reveal what he is thinking. **God used the Logos to reveal His thoughts and to manifest Himself to the world.**

The scriptures recorded in the Bible are "Logos": The message of the Gospel is "Logos." They are expressions of God's **thoughts** and His revealed **will** for man. "Logos" is the "Word of the Lord" or the revealed will of God. **It is the message from the Lord, delivered with His authority and the accompanying power to bring it to pass**.

When Peter preached to the Gentiles at Cornelius' house, he spoke the Word; the "Logos" and "while Peter was still speaking, the Holy Spirit came on all who heard the message" (Acts 10:44). **Peter spoke the Word with authority and God's power accompanied it!**

In Capernaum, the people gathered together in the house where Jesus was staying until there was no more room, "and he preached the Word;" the "Logos" unto them (Mark 2:1-12). Jesus did not read the scriptures from the scroll, He did not give an introduction and He did not preach a sermon based on the scriptures with four points and a few closing remarks. Instead, He preached the "Logos." **He revealed the <u>thoughts</u> and the <u>will</u> of God concerning man through the Words that He spoke and through His actions.**

His words were power as He revealed the will of God! He not only spoke about forgiveness and healing as part of God's will for man, He spoke the word of forgiveness and healing to the sick man with the palsy and he was immediately made whole.

B) The "Logos" is also used to refer to Jesus Christ Himself who is the Living Word. **Jesus as the "Logos" is the personal manifestation of all that God is through a man. In Christ Jesus, the "Logos" is God revealed and manifested not as an impersonal God but one who cares about man and who was willing to come in human flesh to live among men.** This is written in **John 1:1-14:**

> "In the beginning was the Word (Logos) and the Word (Logos) was with God, and the Word (Logos) was God... And the Word (Logos) was made flesh and dwell amount us."

2. "Rhema"

The word **"Rhema"** as used in the New Testament, refers to **"that which is spoken."** It is a word, <u>a promise</u> or <u>an individual scripture</u> that the spirit brings to our remembrance in time of need; a word spoken by God.

The "Rhema" word is active and powerful. Within the "Rhema" word comes the faith needed for its fulfillment. The power for fulfillment of the word is not of us or of our ability: it is of God.

The Apostle Paul encouraged the Ephesians to take "The sword of the Spirit, which is the **Word of God**" in Ephesian 6:17. In this verse, when Paul spoke of the "**Word of God**," he was not referring to the whole Bible but to the "Rhema" word or a scripture the Spirit speaks to your heart and mind. **It is this "Rhema" word which is spoken directly to you from God that becomes a powerful weapon in your mouth.** With it comes the faith that you need to speak out in order to destroy the enemy's strongholds.

When Jesus faced satan in the wilderness, He revealed this powerful strategy. He said, "Man shall not live by bread alone, but by every word that proceeded out of the mouth of God" (Matthew 4:4). **It is this "Rhema" word that God speaks to your spirit that will destroy satan's strongholds not simply repeating verses that you have memorized.**

When the angel told Mary that she would conceive by the Holy Spirit and give birth to the Son of God, it was a "Rhema" word to her. It was a promise from God, spoken by an angel. Along with the "Rhema" word came the faith for its fulfillment. Mary received it and said, "Be it unto me according to thy word" (Luke 1:38). Previously, Mary had questioned the angel by saying, "How can this thing be" but when the angel spoke **a Word from God**, although she did not understand it, she was willing to receive **the Word spoken by God** through the angel.

When Jesus spoke the Word, **"Be Thou clean"** to the leper, it was a "Rhema" word; a promise from God! Again, when Jesus spoke the Word, **"Be opened"** to the man who was deaf and dumb, and when He said to the woman caught in the act of adultery, **"Thy sin be forgiven thee,"** they were "Rhema" words from God being spoken to them.

God may speak the "Rhema" word directly to your spirit or He may speak through another individual. **The "Rhema" word may be a scripture from the written Word or a specific promise from God, just remember that when the "Rhema" word comes to you from God, the power to bring it to pass is contained within it.** When you receive it, all you need to do is simply accept it as Mary did and say, "Be it unto me according to thy Word."

Chapter 6
Warfare Exposed

Anytime you try to obey God in your Christian walk, and you are or feel hindered, diverted or frustrated, it means you are experiencing a spiritual battle. Warfare is a contest or struggle between enemies. A dictionary definition of warfare is as follows:

A state of disharmony or conflict; strife.

Acts undertaken to destroy or undermine the strength of another:

The waging of war against an enemy: ***spiritual warfare***. That is the host of hell and you — the believer.

They have determined to engage and defeat you; a believer in a spiritual battle. As a believer, it is crucial and very important to understand that Satan wants to mangle you (mutilate or disfigure by battering, hacking, cutting, or tearing) in the area of spiritual warfare. Satan purposely assaults you in an attempt to ruin your Christian testimony.

Spiritual warfare must not intimidate you as a believer. Jesus Christ, during His earthly ministry, assured His disciples, saying:

"These things I have spoken unto you, that in me ye might have peace. In the world, ye shall have tribulation: but be of good cheer; I have overcome the world" (John 16:33).

Your confidence and your faith must be based on the Word of God — His assurance to you, and the armor He has provided you for your protection. What you must know in this spiritual warfare is that you are not the "vanquished," but the "victor," and that you have the power to terminate every assignment of the enemy concerning your life, destiny, and your future as well as that of your family. You are destined to succeed and not fail.

You also need to know that as a soldier in the army of the Lord, you must possess the qualities that the Apostle Paul clearly stated:

> **"But thou, O man of God, flee these things; and follow after righteousness, godliness, faith, love, patience, meekness"** (I Timothy 6:11).

You must possess these qualities which range from holiness to meekness, and note that meekness does not mean weakness. Remember the Bible says:

> **"Now the man Moses was very meek, above all the men which were upon the face of the earth"** (Numbers 12:3).

Moses was a powerful man who talked to God face to face, wrought many miracles, and fought and won many battle. Yet, the Bible described him as being meek. Meekness must be sought after by every believer and applied in order for the believer to be sanctified for the Lord's work. Any soldier who does not have these qualities or fruits mentioned by the Apostle Paul, will be wounded on the battlefield by the satanic hosts because he is weak.

When the elements of sin stay incorporated in your daily life, it dilutes and neutralizes the anointing of the Almighty God upon your life. The Bible commands us to:

> **"Love not the world, neither the things that are in the world. If any man love the world, the love of the Father is not in him"** (1 John 2:15).

Paul said:

> **"No man that warreth entangleth himself with the affairs of this life; that he may please him who hath chosen him to be a soldier"** (2 Timothy 2:4).

As you separate yourself from the elements of life — the lust of the flesh, the lust of the eyes, and the pride of life — you learn to walk in righteousness, purity and holiness. Again, the Apostle Paul instructs us to:

> **"Fight the good fight of faith, lay hold on eternal life, whereunto thou art also called, and hast professed a good profession before many witnesses"** (1 Timothy 6:12).

Any soldier, armed with these attributes, is ready to fight offensively.

You may ask, "How can a fight be good?" A fight is "good" when everything is working in your favor: You are living by faith, and God has extended unmeasured and unlimited grace to you on the battlefield. Any soldier in battle, or going to the battlefield, anticipates a good fight of victory when he knows the strategy of the opponent and has the winning ability.

You must " . . . *be strong in the grace that is in Christ Jesus."* **(2 Timothy 2:1).** Every gift that God gives a believer is through His grace or by unmerited favor. Part of the meaning of the word "grace" in Hebrew and Greek is "the protecting and helping favor of God." You need to be strong in the grace released through faith in order to win the war. Until you know how to live in, and practice faith, you will never be able to fight the fight of faith. We are, therefore, admonished accordingly:

"And the things that thou has heard of me among many witnesses, the same commit thou to faithful men, who shall be able to teach others also. Thou therefore endure hardness, as a good soldier of Jesus Christ" (2 Timothy 2:2-3).

Fighting is never a simple task. It entails careful and strategic planning. As a good soldier, you must learn how to endure and persevere through hard situations and circumstances. A well-trained soldier must be able to endure all kinds of hardships. Fighting implies a concentrated action and response on your part. You cannot be idle and expect God to fight for you. He has provided you with the armor and weaponry you need to fight. You must always remember that battles are intense confrontations that demand strength on your part through the medium of prayer. I will be writing about that in the next few chapters.

A good soldier desires to please his commander, or the authority over him, by developing the necessary skills that will make him a better and more qualified fighter. So, likewise, to develop your competence, you must be faithful in your prayer time and in your obedience to God's requests in your life. Discipline, which involves the training needed to develop self-control, character and the ability to accept and submit to authority, cannot be cultivated in one day. It is developed over a period of time.

You must be devoted and committed to the cause of Christ in your life. In the natural realm, the soldier who refuses to increase or become more competent in the use of a gun or sword will be entertaining the chances of being killed on the battlefield. However, the soldier who is persistent in his training, day and night, will be a formidable foe and will conquer the strongest enemy.

Fulfilling the role of a soldier in your Christian journey is a special calling of God. Some believers are weak and hardly ever fight the devil when he is harassing and embarrassing them. Other believers wallow in guilt and condemnation instead of resisting the devil. Some also prefer to accept all the physical, emotional, moral, psychological, and financial problems the devil imposes on them.

Every believer must "count it all joy" to be a soldier in God's army because victory is inevitable and attainable. Remember, the battle is not yours, but the battle belong to our Lord God, Jehovah:

"The LORD is a man of war: the LORD is his name" (Exodus 15:3).

He is not only a God of war, but He is also a devouring and consuming fire according to Hebrews:

"For our God is a consuming fire" (Hebrews 12:29).

A soldier must learn how to persevere, that is, to press on in spite of the difficulties and hardships he faces. You must still continue to press on until the vindication of our God Jehovah prevails. Joseph was able to press on enduring false accusations, hardships, and imprisonment just because of his dreams.

Fellow believer, the devil will attack you because he sees you have a bright future. He will attack you because of your dreams, your God-given destiny, and the height to which God wants to lift you just as He did Joseph. You can go on your knees and fight, and God will take you from the pit to the palace.

Chapter 7
The Aggressive Weapons of Prayer

God will never desert or leave you desolate when you pass through life's fiery trials. Sometimes, when I go through hard and tough times, I pray persistently. I remember some nights when I was provoked by many challenges that forced me to go to a hilltop to pray. I prayed asking God for divine favor and divine intervention. I cried, travailed and agonized in prayers for hours at a time. But the Lord was seemingly silent, not saying anything to me. This was because God was building my faith in Him.

During this time, I never fell victim to condemning thoughts like, "What's wrong? Why should I go through these terrible situations?" because I knew the devil is the accuser of the brethren according to **Revelation 12:10**.

The devil will try to blame every situation on you. He usually starts the battle against you without provocation. You did not choose to enter into battle with the devil, but in the majority of cases, life's obstacles and difficulties are not your choice. Your main challenge is to serve the Lord with sincerity and maintain your determination to win.

Warfare comes in diverse forms. It could be an obstacle of some sort, a difficulty, or pain you experience while attempting to obey God's Word. So many times, God will whisper or speak to my heart and say, "Son, I want you to do this for Me." Suddenly, in the process of trying to obey God's leading and direction, I am besieged with so many difficulties and every possible obstacle would block my path. Yet, I know that I must go on to fulfill God's request. This is how one enters into spiritual warfare. That is why the scriptures say:

> **"For though we walk in the flesh, we do not war after the flesh: (For the weapons of our warfare are not carnal, but mighty through God to the pulling down of strong holds;)"** (2 Corinthians 10:3-4).

Your weapons are not physical guns and bullets. Neither can we win logically or psychologically. Our weapons are spiritual and we win by going down on our knees. In your spiritual warfare, you must therefore enforce your victory by:

> **"Casting down imaginations, and every high thing that exalteth itself against the knowledge of God, and bringing into captivity every thought to the obedience of Christ..."** (2 Corinthians 10:5).

Part of your responsibility is to control your mental faculty in the warfare, and pull down all strongholds of mental stumbling blocks that Satan has thrown at you. A stronghold is any fortified or feeding place or fortress of the devil to outthink and outsmart the purpose and plans of God.

In a spiritual warfare, you must totally depend on God, knowing that the battle is not yours. It belongs to the Lord Almighty who is strong in battle.

> **"Not by might, nor by power, but by my spirit, saith the LORD of hosts"**(Zechariah 4:6).

It is when warfare is done by the Spirit of God that you can confidently say:

"Who are you Satan, before me?" (Zechariah 4:7).

When fighting a battle, you must develop a strategy against your enemy — a strategy based on your knowledge of your enemy's strengths and weaknesses. The Apostle Paul said:

"Lest Satan should get an advantage of us: for we are not ignorant of his devices" (2 Corinthians 2:11).

And Peter warns us, saying:

"Be sober, be vigilant; because your adversary the devil, as a roaring lion, walketh about, seeking whom he may devour: Whom resist stedfast in the faith. . . ." (1 Peter 5:8-9).

Do not allow Satan to astonish, astound, surprise or catch you off guard. So many times, we are sidetracked (even for seemingly legitimate reasons) and because see out of our peripheral vision, we usually do not see him coming. He suddenly attacks us and causes us to loose our ground and/or focus.

The devil knows that his time is short and is at hand. So, it is extremely important now more than ever before for the believer to be sensitive to the Spirit of God and to walk in discernment.

This is so crucial and cannot be over-emphasized. You must have an awareness of spiritual realities and understand that Satan works subtly and systematically. He is tireless in his efforts to cause you to deviate from the plans and purposes of God for your life. That is why being steadfast in faith is very important. It is one of the keys used to silence the roars of the devil.

In the Scriptures, no one displayed or exemplified being steadfast in faith more than Jesus Christ as seen in the fourth chapter of the Book of Matthew. Satan presented Jesus with various temptations to prove His "Son-ship." These temptations ranged from casting Himself down from the temple, to giving Him all power and glory in exchange for His worship of him (Satan). Jesus displayed steadfastness and perseverance by quoting the Word of God back to Satan despite the surrounding difficulties and hardships. He had been on a forty-day fast in the wilderness, but His steadfastness caused the devil to back down for a season **(Matthew 4:1-11)**.

Ephesians 6:11-18 contains crucial equipments that will help you live a victorious Christian life. We are commanded to put on the whole armor of God so that we can stand against the wiles of the devil. The armor is described as:

Having your loins girded about with truth;

Putting on the breastplate of righteousness;

Having your feet shod with the preparation of the Gospel of Peace;

Taking up the shield of faith; and,

Putting on the helmet of salvation, which is the Word of God.

This is the uniform that a soldier in the army of the Lord must wear when wrestling with the four types of spiritual enemies, namely:

(a) *principalities*

(b) *powers*

(c) *rulers of the darkness of this world, and*

(d) *spiritual wickedness in high places*

These non-human enemies are the fallen angels who rule and reign in Satan's realm of authority. I want to give you the definitions and a good understanding of these spiritual enemies that listed above in the following sub-chapters.

(7.1) Principalities

Principalities are the first division of spiritual enemies mentioned. The Greek word for principalities is **KOS-MOSCRATORAS** — a world ruler, an epithet for Satan. Satan is acknowledged as their head. These principalities are princes in Satan's kingdom and have sections or provinces of this world under their control.

The word *principalities* has a special reference in political realms where evil spirits work to influence earthly rulers, kings, presidents, parliaments, legislatures, judges, civil officers, office holders and the entire range of things and men connected with government. The prince of the kingdom of Persia mentioned in the tenth chapter of the book of Daniel is one of these principalities.

When Daniel decided to stand in the gap for the people of Israel to petition God concerning the prophecy spoken by Jeremiah in Daniel Chapter 9, according to the angel that was sent to deliver the answer, his prayer was heard and answered on the very first day that he prayed. The angel (God's messenger), said the prince of Persia withstood (hindered) him for twenty-one days. It took the archangel Michael to rescue him. Only then was he free to go and deliver the message (answered prayer) to Daniel.

This incident is illuminating from several angles. It proves beyond a shadow of doubt that evil angels seek to influence world governments, and wherever possible to hinder God's plans. It also shows that by *persevering prayer*, God's people can defeat the purposes of the enemy.

It is unquestionable that these spirits attack all levels of earthly governments — from main governments to the smallest segments. They seek to manipulate and influence men and women who are in office; whether they realize it or not. Some of the pressure these government officials experience stems from the fact that Satan, and his organized army, try to manipulate them in whatever direction he wants them to go.

Even Christian men who have been placed in governmental positions are not immune from the attacks of these principalities. This explains why, in some instances, they experience difficulty in giving clear-cut solutions to certain issues, or arrive at logical and conclusive decisions on steps to be taken.

The antagonism toward them is not primarily from men who oppose them. Satan is the real source and root of it all.

No wonder we are instructed to pray for those who are in government and in authority over us.

"I exhort therefore, that, first of all, supplications, prayers, intercessions, *and* giving of thanks, be made for all men; For kings, and for all that are in authority; that we may lead a quiet and peaceable life in all godliness and honesty" (1 Timothy 2:1-2).

By doing this, we resist and thwart the effect of the evil one in persuading men to follow the path he has mapped out for them.

(7.2) Powers

The next division of spiritual enemies is Powers. In the Greek translation, the word for *power* is **DUNAMIS** (power, strength, violence, mighty work). This word represents an exceedingly large section of Satan's force that are evil spirits of great energy and force. Their particular method of operation is to attack the personal feelings and thought life of Christians. Unbelievers also come under this form of attack. The terrible crimes we see, read and hear about repeatedly inspired by these evil powers. The method of operation of these powers varies from individual to individual, Christian or unbeliever.

These demons do not exhibit their true colors. They operate under the disguise of self-interest, revenge, self-gratification and so on. These are powerful stimulants for evil beings, which can result in the lowest and foulest of deeds. It is possible that those affected by or exhibiting such actions do not realize that these evil spirits have added their persuasive powers to the base desires inherent in their hearts.

How else do we explain people justifying their evil and cruel actions or course in life as doing the will of God? A case in point is Saul of Tarsus in the book of Acts who went about persecuting Christians before he realized his awful sin against Christ and the people of God. It was not until he was saved that he realized he had been deceived by satanic forces.

As I mentioned earlier, these *powers* attack people's feelings. Left to us, we would not react as violently as we sometimes do when false accusations are made against us or some derogatory remarks are made about us. It is true that we possess the "Adamic" nature which would lead us to resent, and react to such things in the way we do. When our "fleshly" nature is combined with the external stimulations of demons, our negative human reactions are intensified. I am sure that many church quarrels which often last for generations are initiated by these *powers*. This could be the only logical explanation for the deeply-rooted hatred in some churches and among individuals.

Another function of these evil spirits is to defame people's character; hence, we find it easier to speak evil of a person than good. We all sometimes put up defense mechanisms. Our first reaction when something negative is said about us is to rise up to our defense by any means. However, when under the influence of the Holy Spirit, this tendency is reversed, and we then find ourselves doing good rather than evil.

In addition to the above, these evil spirits stir up unrest and chaos in families and among human beings in general.

Part of their nefarious (evil) work includes raising talebearers among brethren. From the scriptures, we know that Satan is called the "accuser of the brethren," yet, for example, nine times out of ten, when Christians are at loggerheads, and they lay down the facts, they often find out that there was really no logical reason for the bickering and unpleasantness toward each other in the first place.

It is true that bad feelings and unpleasantness among Christians should not exist, but the sad reality is that they often do and usually for no good reason at all, even from a worldly person's point of view.

Let us face these issues squarely because these *powers* are working tirelessly to destroy the peace in the lives of God's people. This, apparently, is their particular assignment. So, they work hard at it.

(7.3) Rulers of the Darkness of this World

The evil spirits that fall under this category are those who foster superstition, fortune-telling, and false teachings of various kinds. They delude people into watching out for "signs" and cause people to yield to, or follow signs. They make mental suggestions and/or emotional impressions and the people receive these signs and suggestions regardless of their source.

The Holy Spirit is the only One that can interpret the Word of God and write it into our hearts. The vast multitudes in this world today, even our so-called civilized countries, are highly superstitious. The sight of a black cat frightens some people and many will look at horseshoes as objects of good luck.

These illustrations only touch the fringe of the superstition that holds untold millions in spiritual slavery. You must remember that your enemies are not human. Friends, spouses, relatives and even political leaders are not your "problem." Satan may capitalize on their weaknesses and use them to harass or hurt you in his attempt to remove your focus away from God. He wants you to fight on the human level by walking in strife and un-forgiveness. His primary goal is to move you out of the area of God's purpose, power and protection into a carnal battle.

God has destined you to succeed and to have victory over satanic plans and agenda, but you must be willing to totally depend and rely upon the armor and weapons that God has provided. This is the only way you can overrule, override and overtake satanic propaganda and principles. The eternal blood of Jesus Christ is a very powerful weapon that God has given us and it is one of the ways that you gain the upper hand over satan and his evil forces. The Bible says **Revelation 12:11** that believers overcome the devil by the blood of Jesus.

"... They overcame him by the blood of the Lamb, and by the word of their testimony ..."

You are a victor from the foundations of the earth. Therefore, you are not qualified to be a loser and/or failure.

(7.4) Wicked Spirits in Heavenly Places

The fourth group is *wicked spirits in heavenly places* which is an accurate translation of the expression *spiritual wickedness in high places.* These wicked spirits are religious demons that intrude into the highest religious experiences. They come as "angels of light," sometimes speaking through men of the pulpits, giving these unregenerate men false ideas that have caused them to lead many people astray in the past and in recent times.

This is especially true where modernism and higher criticism have taken over. We see their handiwork in such cults as Jehovah's Witnesses whose devotees tell us that the first Greek words mean so and so; yet, these witnesses do not know the first thing about Greek. In order to substantiate their unbiblical teachings, they seek to change the meaning of some words. Some of these evil spirits pose as the Holy Spirit Himself.

Many earnest people have been drawn into such movements through ignorance and have thereby been exposed to the worst types of demonic practices. These wicked spirits are referred to as religious spirits. Their special sphere of operation is in the heavenly places which for one thing includes the very air around us.

Ephesians 2:2 states that Satan is "the prince of the power of the air." It is these evil spirits that ensure that certain people join churches but remain unsaved. They get baptized and profess religion (as opposed to salvation) and a kind of holiness. They sometimes share their marvelous dreams and ecstasies, give prophesies and they lay claims to having spiritual gifts. Yet, they remain unsaved.

Raphael Grant

One of the programs of these evil spirits is to attack these conscientious and religious people and get them to accept heresies and false impressions to a point where they become self-conceited and self-righteous, placing themselves above others. The Pharisees and Scribes were very religious, but they were described thus:

> **"Ye are of your father the devil . . ."** (John 8:44).

> **". . . O full of all subtlety and all mischief, thou child of the devil,** thou **enemy of all righteousness . . ."** (Acts 13:10).

> **"He that committeth sin is of the devil. . ."** (1 John 3:8).

The same book of **1 John 5:9** states:

> **"And we know that we are of God, and the whole world lieth in wickedness."** (1 John 5:9).

A man can only be in one of two places: Either in the hands of Jesus or in the hand of the wicked one. Satan's kingdom, therefore, consists of angels, demons, and men on earth who do his bidding:

> **"But in all of this, we are more than conquerors through Jesus Christ our Lord"** (Romans 8:37).

Jesus said:

> **"Behold, I give unto you power to tread on serpents and scorpions, and over all the power of the enemy: and nothing shall by any means hurt you"** (Luke 10:19).

The Apostle Paul also said:

> "That at the name of Jesus every knee should bow, of things in heaven, and things in earth, and things under the earth; And that every tongue should confess that Jesus Christ is Lord, to the glory of God the Father" (Phillipians 2:10-11).

> "For our God is a consuming fire" (Hebrews 12:29).

Our Lord God is described thus:

> The Lord is a man of war: the LORD is his name" (Exodus 15:3).

God is the One who created and formed you; so He knows your limitations. He commanded you not to be fearful:

> "But now thus saith the LORD that created thee, O Jacob, and he that formed thee, O Israel, Fear not: for I have redeemed thee, I have called thee by thy name; thou art mine. When thou passest through the waters, I will be with thee; and through the rivers, they shall not overflow thee: when thou walkest through the fire, thou shalt not be burned; neither shall the flame kindle upon thee" (Isaiah 43:1-2).

He will protect and carry you through every battle. You are not a unique case in God's kingdom. Satan afflicts and tests all saints everywhere. Remember what the Apostle Paul said:

> "Be sober, be vigilant; because your adversary the devil, as a roaring lion, walketh about, seeking whom

he may devour: Whom resist stedfast in the faith, knowing that the same afflictions are accomplished in your brethren that are in the world" (1 Peter 5:8-9).

Sometimes, the problems you face tend to isolate you and make you feel sorry for yourself, thinking that God has His favorite children who are free from life's struggles. That is a lie of the devil and is aimed at causing jealousy and division in the body of Christ. Every individual has struggles and temptations because the enemy roams the earth seeking people to devour.

"There hath no temptation taken you but such as is common to man: but God is faithful, who will not suffer you to be tempted above that ye are able; but will with the temptation also make a way to escape, that ye may be able to bear it" (1 Corinthians 10:13).

God's power is always greater than Satan's power. So, victory is assured.

Chapter 8
The Raising of an Apostolic Generation

A new breed of the apostolic generation is being raised for the propagation of the Gospel to the entire world as a witness before the return of our Lord Jesus Christ. As such, we need an apostolic anointing for the apostolic anointing is the finishing anointing. The scriptures say:

> **"Jesus saith unto them, My meat is to do the will of Him that sent Me, and to finish His work"** (John 4:34).

Such statements or declarations by Jesus are known as apostolic verses or proclamations. The Holy Spirit is all five in one: apostolic, prophetic, evangelistic, teacher and pastor.

The Holy Spirit is an **evangelist Spirit** because He convicts sinners and draws them to Christ. You cannot be a Christian if you have not been convicted by the Holy Spirit.

The Holy Spirit is a **pastoral Spirit.** In the book of Acts of the Apostles, the Apostle Paul told the Ephesians to feed the flock of God over which the Holy Spirit has made them overseers. You cannot be an overseer unless the Holy Spirit has made you one.

The Holy Spirit is the One who ordains pastors.

The Holy Spirit is a **teacher.** The Bible makes us understand that "when He has come, He will teach us all things."

The Holy Spirit is a prophetic Spirit.

The Holy Spirit is an apostolic Spirit because He is sent. The Greek word for apostle is *apostolos* which means the **sent one** or one that is **sent on a mission.**

God sends evangelists, prophets, pastors, and teachers. However, by definition, an apostle implies one who has been sent on a mission by God. Jesus told His disciples that after He has gone to the Father, the Father would send the Holy Spirit or the Comforter in His name (**John 14:16, 26**). The Holy Spirit, therefore, is a sent Spirit and an apostolic Spirit. Jesus Christ, as we know, also walked in the prophetic, apostolic, pastoral, teaching and evangelistic anointing or calling. The Bible says the Spirit of Christ is the spirit of prophecy. The Father is everything that the Holy Spirit is:

<u>*God is an evangelistic God*</u>: When Adam sinned, it was God who came to the garden searching for him, saying:

> **"Adam, where art thou?"** (Genesis 3:8-9).

<u>*God is a teaching God*</u> because He is always teaching His children through direct instructions, situations and circumstances of life, and through His Word.

<u>*God is a pastoral God.*</u> David said of Him in **Psalm 23**:

> **"The LORD is my shepherd; I shall not want"** (Psalm 23:1).

<u>*God is a prophetic God*</u> because He does nothing without first revealing it to His servants, the prophets according

to **Amos 3:7**. Every time God wants to do a thing, He always needs somebody to prophesy the message before He brings it to pass.

God is an apostolic God because He sends His people. He sent Jesus to die on the cross to redeem man from sin and bring reconciliation between man and God. Jesus said to His disciples:

> ". . . As my Father hath sent me, even so send I you" (John 20:21).

It was God who sent John the Baptist to prepare the way for the Messiah, and it was God who sent the prophets of old.

Part of God's divine being and nature is apostolic, and so God the Father, God the Son and God the Holy Spirit are one. In these last days, God is raising apostles and putting on them the mantles of apostolic anointing which is the finishing anointing. It is the same anointing that will bring Jesus back as King of Kings and Lord of Lords. **Every unfinished business will be finished because of the apostolic anointing.**

The first century Church claimed its world (its day and time) for Christ without even having or holding a Bible. There were no cars or airplanes in its day, but it took the Gospel of Christ to its world with mighty manifestations of power.

The Word was also preached not by "enticing words of man's wisdom," but in the demonstration of the Spirit and of power. This means that the faith of the people of God who heard the Word of God was not based on the wisdom of men but in the power of God.

The Apostle Peter was once in a meeting where the crowd was so thick, and the needs of the people were so great. God saw that Peter could not handle the situation alone. Among this crowd were sick people in need of healing. God, therefore, transferred some of His anointing into Peter's shadow so that while ministering to and healing people on his right hand side, his shadow fell on his left hand side, healing as many people as it touched.

The Apostle Paul was also in a large meeting where so many people had gathered that he was not able to lay hands on everybody. To resolve this situation, aprons and handkerchiefs were put on his body and then laid on those who were sick. They were instantly healed. These are some of the manifestations wrought by the hands of the apostles. These manifestations are returning to the body of Christ.

The early apostles understood prayer and had insight into the Word of God. Peter said:

> **"Wherefore, brethren, look ye out among you seven men of honest report, full of the Holy Ghost and wisdom, whom we may appoint over this business. But will give ourselves continually to prayer, and to the ministry of the word"** (Acts 6:3-4).

The early church knew the importance of the "upper room," but today's modern church has turned the upper room into a supper room.

> **"And when they had prayed, the place was shaken where they were assembled together..."** (Acts 4:31).

Today, when we pray, the place is taken.

When the apostles died, the church went into ceremonialism, tradition, and seclusion of some so-called *holy people* to whom the Bible was given so that they could read it and tell others what it says. The apostolic spirit, therefore, died in the church and people said miracles were no longer for today; suggesting that we could live without it. The church has been on earth for two thousand years and still has unfinished business to clear up. Two thousand years is a long time. There are entire groups and nations who have never heard the Gospel of Jesus Christ preached to them — not even once!

I would like you to know that God is supernaturally mobilizing His end-time harvesters. We are in a time when we, the body of Christ, the Church of God, urgently need the apostolic spirit to be able to complete the mission that God has given to us before Christ returns:

> **"And this gospel of the kingdom shall be preached in all the world for a witness unto all nations; and then shall the end come"** (Matthew 24:14).

Beloved, none of the signs of the end time as listed in **Matthew 24:12** will bring Christ back except the preaching of the Gospel of Christ to every creature. There are six billion people on earth, but only three billion have heard the Gospel of Jesus. The other three billion are yet to hear, even for the first time, the Gospel of Jesus Christ.

According to the United States Center for World Missions, there are still two and a half billion people in the world who constitute more than 16,000 ethnic groups. An ethnic group is a people that has its own language, culture and tradition, etc.

There are thousands of preachers in Kenya. It takes only a few hours to get to Somalia. However, the majority of the population of Somalia and the population of many other tribes worldwide have never been reached with the Gospel of Jesus Christ.

There are hundreds of missionaries in Kenya, and there are between two hundred and two hundred and fifty Pentecostal churches in Nairobi alone. Yet, there are more than forty tribes in Kenya that have never heard the Gospel of Jesus Christ.

Chapter 9
Revival Cry in the Globe

There shall be revival in every home, community, city, and nation. This revival will be inexplicable because it will bring about the conviction of sin to men — deep conviction of sin. The church of God will also get back to its first course — prayer; prayer for the perishing souls that have not yet been reached by the Gospel of Jesus. The church will also pray for the outpouring of the Holy Spirit, which will bring conviction of souls.

Historically, all of the great revivals in the past were marked and birthed by deep and powerful convictions of sin. During this period of revival, there were instances of people being so uncoordinated that they could not drive their cars home because of a deep conviction of their sins by the Holy Spirit. There were also circumstances where people were seen trembling from head to toe that they would fall to their knees because they were under such deep and powerful conviction of sin.

The Spirit of God was present at these meetings in great power, convicting people. This was not emotionalism, but a deep conviction of sin by the Spirit of God. But all these happened as a result of a different level of prayer. There shall be the preaching of salvation through Jesus Christ or the law of God in the scriptures. The Bible says:

"But we know that the law *is* good, if a man use it lawfully" (1 Timothy 1:8).

Here, it says that the law is good, but in verse 11, it says:

"According to the glorious gospel of the blessed God, which was committed to my trust" (1 Timothy 1:11).

Here, he uses the glorious gospel without preaching the good law, which is the salvation of our God, and righteousness which brings conviction of sin. As such, the Holy Ghost must have some tracks to run on, so He runs on the Word of God. If we preach the law, the Spirit will bless it and help people to see the reality of sin.

Chapter 10
Demonstration is Witness

Every preacher must be a demonstrator; if not, he/she should forget about preaching. The whole world is waiting for the proclamation of the gospel with the demonstration of the Spirit and of power. The Apostle Paul said:

> "And my speech and my preaching was not with enticing words of man's wisdom, but in **demonstration of the Spirit and of power:** That your faith should not stand in the wisdom of men, but in the **power of God**" (1 Corinthians 2:4-5).

God is a God of demonstration and evidence. Morris Cerullo once said: "God is 'PROOF' and His children are 'PROOF PRODUCERS.'" Therefore, if you preach or are a minister of the Gospel of Christ, and you cannot provide proof, evidence, or demonstrate of what you preach, then you are not qualified to be a minister of the gospel:

> **"But ye shall receive power, after that the Holy Ghost is come upon you: and ye shall be witnesses unto me both in Jerusalem, and in all Judea, and in Samaria, and unto the uttermost part of the earth"** (Acts 1:8).

According to the Greek translation, the word **power**, as mentioned above, refers to **power in action;** for example, performing miracles, ability, mighty works, energy, etc. It can also be described as a supernatural force. The Greek word for power is **dunamis.** The English word for power as derived from the Greek is **dynamite.**

The word *witness* comes from the Greek word *"martyr."* According to Greek authority, *"martyr"* denotes one who can vouch for, guarantee, verify, or prove what he has seen, heard, known, etc. Many *witnesses* laid down their lives for their testimony about Jesus Christ that the word *"martyr"* gradually became synonymous with "one who bears witness by his death." This eventually became the meaning of the word "martyr" when translated into the English language. The original meaning, however, was *witness*.

The word "witness" is defined as:

To give evidence

One who furnishes evidence

Proof

One who demonstrates, substantiates or verifies his testimony with an exhibition of evidence.

Jesus said:

". . . ye shall receive power, after that the Holy Ghost is come upon you: and ye shall be witnesses unto me . . ." (Acts 1:8).

What was Jesus saying in this passage? He was saying that after the Holy Ghost has come upon you, and you are endued with power, you should produce proof, evidence and/or verify your testimony about Him. All the apostles were "proof producers." They verified their testimony and guaranteed what they preached.

For example, Peter, through the power of the Holy Spirit, healed a crippled man at the gate of the temple called Beautiful and was subsequently arrested. Before his arrest, while testifying to the crowd, he declared:

> " . . . we are His witnesses" (Acts 3:15).

In his testimony of Jesus, Stephen (the martyr) also mentioned:

> " . . . the tabernacle of witness in the wilderness . . ." (Acts 7:44).

The magnificent tent of Israel was called the "Tabernacle of Witness" because, for twenty-four hours of everyday, there was proof, evidence and verification of God's presence and miraculous power there:

> "And this gospel of the kingdom shall be preached in all the world for a witness unto all nations; and then shall the end come" (Matthew 24:14).

Many who preach sermons and discourses, but have not their sermons empowered by the Holy Ghost, lack the ability to witness with proof. But those who are His "Tabernacle of Witness" are *"proof producers"* because for twenty-four hours of everyday of their lives, the miraculous power of God is present within them.

It is one thing to be a minister, church member, deacon or preacher, but it is another thing to be able to say, "I am His witness." Regarding this great salvation, the book of Hebrews declares:

> " . . . which at the first began to be spoken by the Lord, and was confirmed unto us by them that heard him; God also <u>bearing them witness, both with signs and</u>

wonders, and with divers miracles, and gifts of the Holy Ghost . . ." (Hebrews 2:3-4).

The gospel was with evidence while the message was with proof as shown in **Acts 2:22**. God the Father anointed, equipped and sent the Lord Jesus into the world and as such, Jesus was:

"...approved of God . . . by miracles, wonders and signs... " (Acts 2:22).

We see this stated again in **Acts 10:38**:

"God anointed Him with the Holy Ghost and with power."

"Then Philip went down to the city of Samaria, and preached Christ unto them. And the people with one accord gave heed unto those things which Philip spake, hearing and seeing the miracles which he did. For unclean spirits, crying with loud voice, came out of many that were possessed *with them*: and many taken with palsies, and that were lame, were healed. And there was great joy in that city" (Acts 8:5-8).

He testified about Christ with evidential proof because he was a witness and the power of the Holy Ghost was inside of him. T. L. Osborn, in his excellent book **"THE PROMISE OF PENTECOST,"** said:

"The witness who produces evidence in the court is the one who wins the case."

Therefore, the preacher who produces evidence wherever he stands to testify and witness about the resurrection of Christ, is the one who wins the world for Christ.

"O God, raise up witnesses for we don't need eloquent, flamboyant or decorative messages or preachers.

But Father, we need witnesses to produce evidential proof to this world of sin and problems.

Where are the documented evidence of the first century church or the early church which caused them to turn the world upside down for Christ; which caused Peter to tell the lame man at the gate of the Temple called Beautiful,

"Silver and gold have I none; but such as I have give I thee: In the name of Jesus Christ of Nazareth rise up and walk. And he took him by the right hand, and lifted him up: and immediately his feet and ankle bones received strength" *(Acts 3:6-7).*

Father, the witness — the evidential proof — is lost in today's modern day church and is more concerned with competition, envy, get-rich-quick schemes and the number or size of his church membership or congregation.

O God, heal the modern day church of its powerlessness and inability to witness — produce evidential proof — and let there be a restoration of the first century church witness, that we may flood heaven with people that bear the mark of Christ."

The whole world is waiting for a gospel that will be preached with evidential proof:

"Stephen, full of faith and power, did great wonders and miracles among the people . . . and all that sat in the council, looking steadfastly on him, saw his face as it had been the face of an angel" (Acts 6:8, 15).

Stephen was a witness. His preaching was with power, and he was full of the Holy Ghost. O that God will raise up Stephen(s), Peter(s), Philip(s) and Paul(s) in our generation today that will be witnesses:

"And when they had prayed, the place was shaken where they were assembled together; and they were all filled with the Holy Ghost, and they spake the word of God with boldness. And the multitude of them that believed were of one heart and of one soul: neither said any of *them* that aught of the things which he possessed was his own; but they had all things common. And with great power gave the apostles witness of the resurrection of the Lord Jesus: and great grace was upon them all" (Acts 4:31-33).

Why were multitudes added to the early church? They were added to the early church because of the signs and wonders. These apostles preached with evidence!

Chapter 11
Another Level of Prayer

As I stated in the Preface of this book, there are levels of payer. It is one thing to pray and another thing to pray (at) another level of prayer. As a matter of fact, no prayer is ordinary. When you pray another level of prayer, you get another level of result, and when you pray ordinary prayers, you get ordinary results. Another level of prayer transcends and supersedes the laws of nature. It is a prayer that comes before God as a "white flame."

God is a God of plan, regularity and power. We call His normal way of working *"Laws of Nature."* Lower laws serve the purpose for higher laws and when harmonized, are transcended by higher laws. The laws in the Bible and life can transcend the law governing matter. These, in turn, may serve the laws of psychology. Moral laws transcend physical laws, and another level of prayer, which is spiritual law, transcends them all, even the law of gravity.

According to the law of gravity, anything that goes up must come down. However, another level of prayer is so forceful that the force of gravity cannot withstand it and nothing else can hinder, thwart or stop it because it is unstoppable.

In **Joshua Chapter 10**, Joshua prayed and the heavenly bodies were made subject to his prayer. A prolonged battle was going on between the Israelites and their enemies and night was rapidly approaching. Joshua realized that a few more hours of daylight was needed to ensure victory for the Lord's host. So, Joshua; that sturdy man of God, stepped into the breach with another level of prayer. Since the sun was rapidly declining into the west of God's people to reap the full fruits of a noted victory, Joshua lifted up his eyes to heaven and cried out in the sight and hearing of Israel.

To paraphrase, he said: *"God, I want to do something that has never been done before so that I will become the first point of reference."* God asked him what it was that he wanted to do, and Joshua replied that he wanted to violate the laws of nature. God gave him the go ahead to ask. Joshua said: *"I need the sunlight for twenty-four hours for a total victory."*

God then turned to look at His Son, Jesus Christ on His right hand side, the Holy Ghost, the twelve elders (sons of Jacob), and the angelic host, and asked: *"What do you think?"* Joshua, still standing in the midst of the battle, pushed his case further by saying: *"Father, you cannot deny me this request."* At this point, the Eternal Word (Jesus Christ), the Holy Ghost, the twelve elders and the angelic host said to God: *"Father, You are the Big Boss."* So God looked at Joshua and said, *"permission granted."*

Joshua then looked up and said: *"Sun, stand thou still upon Gibeon; and thou, Moon, in the valley of Ajalon"* until further notice. And the sun actually stood still, and the moon stopped in its course at the command of this praying man who prayed another level of prayer until the Lord's people had avenged themselves on the Lord's enemies. The scripture says:

"And there was no day like that before it or after it, that the LORD hearkened unto the voice of man…" (Joshua 10:14).

Scientists have concluded that there is a day missing in creation. This day happens to be the day mentioned above. Another level of prayer renounces the natural and invokes the supernatural for the impossible to take place. This kind of prayer avails when every thing else fails.

Moses was a man that prayed another level of prayer. As a matter of fact, Moses was a radical prayer warrior who prayed radical prayers. Below is an example of one of his many prayers:

"And Moses returned unto the LORD, and said, Oh, this people have sinned a great sin, and have made them gods of gold. Yet now, if thou wilt forgive their sin--; and if not, blot me, I pray thee, out of thy book which thou has written. And the LORD said to Moses, Whosoever hath sinned against me, him will I blot out of my book" (Exodus 32:31-33).

This is another level of prayer; for a man to stand before Jehovah (in intercession) and tell Him that if He will not forgive the sins of His people, He should blot his name out of the Book of Life. This is a dangerous prayer to make and it takes people of faith, courage and boldness to pray such a prayer. Moses talked to God face to face and had the boldest and most unhindered access to God.

Importunity is another level of prayer and it brings familiarity and closeness to God. It also gives relish, frequency, point and potency to prayer. It is the only kind of prayer that moves God to act in our favor. In the book of Exodus, we read more accounts of another level of prayer:

"And the LORD said unto Moses, I have seen this people, and, behold, it is a stiff-necked people: Now therefore let Me alone, that My wrath may wax hot against them, and that I may consume them: and I will make of thee a great nation" (Exodus 32:9-10).

Upon hearing what the Lord said, Moses employed the power of attorney and intercession before Jehovah God and began to reason with God on certain facts and truths.

"And Moses besought the LORD his God, and said, LORD, why doth Thy wrath wax hot against Thy people, which Thou hast brought forth out of the land of Egypt with great power, and with a mighty hand? Wherefore should the Egyptians speak, and say, For mischief did He bring them out, to slay them in the mountains, and to consume them from the face of the earth? Turn from Thy fierce wrath, and repent of this evil against Thy people. Remember Abraham, Isaac, and Israel, Thy servants, to whom thou swarest by Thine Own self, and saidst unto them, I will multiply your seed as the stars of heaven, and all this land that I have spoken of will I give unto your seed, and they shall inherit it for ever" (Exodus 32:11-13).

This made it impossible for God to resist or deny the prayer of Moses, the mighty intercessor. After such indubitable and indomitable prayer, the Bible records:

"And the LORD repented of the evil which he thought to do unto his people" (Exodus 32:14).

There are governmental and constitutional laws that govern nature and laws that govern matter, psychology and the force of gravity, but there is a higher law that superimposes itself and its influence over all these laws. It is stronger, inflexible and inexorable above any other law or decree. This decree simply states: *Call Upon Me and I will answer You."*

"He shall call upon me, and I will answer him . . ." (Psalm 91:15).

Prayer is capable of changing the mind of God. When Hezekiah, the praying King was sick, God sent Prophet Isaiah to warn him of his approaching end and to put all his affairs in order because of his impending death.

"In those days was Hezekiah sick unto death. And the prophet Isaiah the son of Amos came to him, and said unto him, Thus saith the LORD, Set thine house in order; for thou shalt die, and not live" (2 Kings 20:1).

The decree that he will die came directly from God. Who can turn aside or reverse what God Himself has decreed? Immediately and without delay, Hezekiah appealed to God:

"Then he turned his face to the wall, and prayed unto the LORD, saying, I beseech Thee, O LORD, remember now how I have walked before Thee in truth and with a perfect heart, and have done that which is good in Thy sight. And Hezekiah wept sore" (2 Kings 20:2-3).

While Hezekiah was praying, the Prophet Isaiah was already on his way home. Hezekiah had barely finished praying when

God gave Prophet Isaiah another message for him. This time, the message was pleasant and encouraging.

Prayers can change the mind of God. Hezekiah's prayer affected God and God changed His verdict. Prayers have unlimited potency and capabilities before God. Where are the praying men that will pray for incredible results?:

> **"And it came to pass, before Isaiah was gone out into the middle court, that the world of the LORD came to him, saying, Turn again, and tell Hezekiah the captain of My people, Thus saith the LORD, the God of David thy father, I have heard thy prayer, I have seen thy tears: behold, I will heal thee: on the third day thou shalt go up unto the house of the LORD. And I will add unto thy days fifteen years; and I will deliver thee and this city out of the hand of the king of Assyria; and I will defend this city for Mine Own sake, and for My servant David's sake"** (2 Kings 20:4-6).

Prayer is effectual and becomes another level when it is offered up with an agony of desire. The Apostle Paul speaks of it as "travail of the soul." Jesus Christ, when praying in the garden of Gethsemane, was in so much agony that His sweat was like drops of blood:

> **"And being in an agony he prayed more earnestly: and his sweat was as it were great drops of blood falling down to the ground"** (Luke 22:44).

Another level of prayer is when you agonize in prayers for hours till your strength is gone and you are completely exhausted. Such prayers prevail with God.

Jonah fled from duty and took a ship heading for a distant port, but God followed him. By a strange providence, this disobedient prophet whom God had sent to Nineveh, was cast out of the vessel and swallowed up by a fish which God had prepared. In the belly of the fish, he cried out to God against whom he had sinned. God intervened and caused the fish to vomit him out on to dry land. Even the fishes of the great deep are subject to the laws of another level of prayer.

Likewise, Elijah foretold Ahab the King of the impending drought. During this period, food and water would become scarce. After Elijah prayed on another level, the heavens were shut and there was no rain for three and a half years. He also prayed down fire from heaven on Mount Carmel which made the people of Israel declare: *"The Lord, He is God."* Elijah later prayed again:

> **"And Elijah said unto Ahab, Get thee up, eat and drink; for there is a sound of abundance of rain"** (1 Kings 18:41).

Prayer is profoundly simple, and simply profound. "Prayer is the simplest form of speech that infant lips can try," and yet so sublime that it outranges all speech and exhausts man's vocabulary. God turned the organizers to agonize in prayer. Leonard Raevenhill said: "We can preach and perish, but we cannot pray and perish.

The great scientist, Albert Einstein, first predicted the possibilities of the atom in 1905 when he worked out the mathematical formula which forecasted its incredible power. By the time World War II broke out in its fury, scientists had mastered the secrets of the atomic chain reaction. But, as World War II came to an end, an event took place which caused the countenance of men to pale in fear: the discovery and harnessing of the power of the atom. Hiroshima and Nagasaki melted in the fervent heat of the terrible holocaust caused by the atomic bomb.

Yet, as the World War II ended, America was snugly relaxed in the complacent belief that she alone possessed the secret of the bomb. Four years passed and the country was rudely awakened. Russia, aided by traitors to the U.S., stole atomic secrets from the U.S. and learned to make the bomb.

On August 20, 1953 came the fateful announcement that Russia had exploded a hydrogen bomb. The H-Bomb is believed to have a thousand times the power of an atomic bomb and can easily destroy everything within a ten-mile radius. It is potentially capable of destroying, in a minute, the world's largest cities like Paris or New York.

There is more power locked in prayers than in an atomic bomb. Russia possesses hydrogen bombs or H-Bombs, but we possess P-Bombs or prayer bombs which are more powerful, fearful and dangerous compared to the hydrogen bomb.

The hydrogen bomb can utterly destroy the world's largest cities in a minute, but prayers can within seconds, turn the whole universe upside down for Jesus. Prayers can totally annihilate and destroy the kingdom and works of the devil within the twinkle of an eye. Prayers are more powerful than the modern day weapons that have been improved upon by computer technology, and more dangerous than inter-continental ballistic missiles.

God is raising prayer warriors of another level of prayer who will pray as though God is God and Satan is Satan. If believers can see the invisible power of prayer, they can do the impossible. We don't need intellectual power. What we need is more spiritual power. The devil's number one tool is not an active sinner, but an inactive Christian.

Praying people get results. God is looking for people who agonize in prayers. He is not looking for organizers. It is time for the church or the body of Christ to stop praying ordinary and normal prayers and move on to another level of prayers that is eccentric, exceptional, extraordinary, rare, strange, striking, unusual, and distinctive and this comes as a result of much travailing, prevailing and agonizing.

God is raising an army of people who are persistent, enduring, immovable, indefatigable, lasting and persevering in prayers because they are steady and have a "holy stubbornness" in prayers. In the Bible, Ezra was a praying reformer who understood and had knowledge of extraordinary and distinctive prayers. He had returned from Babylon under the patronage of the king of Babylon who was strangely 'moved' toward Ezra and favored him in many ways.

Ezra had been in Jerusalem for a few days when the princes came to him with the distressing information that the people of Israel had not separated themselves from the people of that country and were partaking in the abominations of the heathen nations around them. Worst of all, the princes and rulers of Israel were at the forefront of these abominable acts.

This was the saddest news Ezra had ever received. He did not know what to do about the situation, especially since the "church" i.e., the people of God were hopelessly involved in the ways of the "world." He found that the Levites, princes and people of God were intermarrying, forming close and sacred family ties, and having social and business lives with the Gentile nations — a violation of the laws of God.

Ezra, being a man of prayers, was deeply moved by this situation so he began to fast and pray. He lay prostrate on the ground before God weeping and praying. The whole city united with him in prayers. This is another level of prayer — the only way to placate God:

> **"Now when Ezra had prayed, and when he had confessed, weeping and casting himself down before the house of God, there assembled unto him out of Israel a very great congregation of men and women and children: for the people wept very sore"** (Ezra 10:1).

Daniel, the praying captive, understood that the desolation of Jerusalem would be accomplished in seventy years as declared by the Word of the Lord through Prophet Jeremiah **(Daniel 9:2)**. And the Bible records:

> **"And I set my face unto the Lord God, to seek by prayer and supplications, with fasting, and sackcloth, and ashes: And I prayed unto the LORD my God ..."** (Daniel 9:3-4).

There is nothing like seeking the face of the Lord in prayer with supplication and fasting. Many pray to their 'gods' but we pray to the Almighty God as Daniel did. The prayer of Daniel is another level of prayer. It provoked heaven and stirred up Jehovah to vindicate and deliver His people. The Bible says that, " . . . on the first day that he (Daniel) set his heart to understand and chasten himself before his God, his words were heard . . ."

"<u>At the beginning of thy supplications</u> the commandment came forth, and I am come to shew thee; for thou art greatly beloved: therefore understand the matter, and consider the vision" (Daniel 9:23).

Another level of prayer is the prayer that is not heard on the second or third day, but is always heard by God on the first day for a quick and speedy answer, and the answer is unstoppable. In fact, no prince of Persia can stop the answer because the prayers are too powerful for the answer to be held back by principalities and powers. What men cannot do, prayer does.

Another level of prayer brings victory to losers and success to those who would otherwise fail. It makes cowards courageous and can bring high hopes to those given to depression. Those who pray on another level of prayer consider things on a divine dimension. Their strength may be limited, but they understand that God's power is unlimited. Their abilities may be few, but on another level of prayer, they know God can do all things.

The Bible records that "there was one Anna, a prophetess," and this suggests that she was not well known. Yet she prayed prayers that affected eternity and brought God to earth to take human nature and bring reconciliation between Him and mankind:

"And there was one Anna, a prophetess, the daughter of Phanuel, of the tribe of Aser: she was of a great age, and had lived with an husband seven years from her virginity; And she was a widow of about fourscore and four years, which departed not from the temple, but served God with fastings and prayers night and day. And she coming in that instant gave thanks likewise unto the Lord, and spake of him to all them that looked for redemption in Jerusalem" (Luke 2:36-38).

It is one thing to pray, but it is another thing to pray on another level of prayer. This woman that gave herself to prayers with fasting, even at more than 84 years of age, was heaven-bound. Oh that God will raise women who will pray like Anna, the praying prophetess. Where are the militant prayer warriors who knew nothing other than prayers? I prayed a prayer sometime ago: "God, let me become a prayer, that prayer will become me."

When you pray and become a walking prayer offered up in Jesus' name, your presence will affect the evil one, change events, and help the advancement of God's plans. When you pray and become a prayer, your mere presence will be recognized by evil spirits and by the Almighty God Himself. When you are a prayer, the effect of your presence is precisely the same as a prayer on another level. I am waiting for a time in my life when I will become such a prayer that when the word 'prayer' is mentioned, I will turn around and reply, "yes, sir!" This could be you also.

God, raise up people who will shun publicity to seek Your face in the privacy of their closets. As the unborn baby encumbers the body of its mother, so may the growing "body" of prayer and soul-travail dislocate from the church and locate its authority in Jesus Christ, the Son of the living God.

Paul and Silas dynamited the prison walls with prayer. Since we have substituted traveling for travailing, we have no births. He who kneels before God will stand in any situation; and he who fears God fears no man. That which is born in prayer will survive any test. We need "knights" of prayers to lead "nights of prayers." The church began with the men in the *"upper room"* agonizing; but today, the church is ending up with "men in the supper room" organizing.

Prayer is the womb of the embodiment of grace, and there is no total remedy as the sovereign remedy of prayer. The apostles prayed on another level of prayer. If the body of Christ will return to the apostolic practice waiting on the Lord for "apostolic power," we could then go on to "apostolic possibilities." When praying on another level of prayer, man is linked with God in intimacy and the devil is baffled and beaten.

As the first atomic bomb shook Hiroshima, so, praying on another level alone can release the power that will shake the hearts of men. Prayer is not a defense mechanism against the wiles of the devil but a weapon among weapons. Prayer is a time-eater. In the fundamental stages, the clock seems to drag; but as the heart and soul get used to the holy exercise, time flies when praying. If we will have a great standing with God, we will have less standing with men. If prayer decays in the church of Christ, revival will delay, and Satan and hell will have no fear of praying men.

Lord, I give You thanks for the army that consists of continent shakers, nation shakers, and world shakers. This army of believers will not fail because they have been tested and approved. God has allowed the devil to shake them so that those things that are shakable will be shaken off, and the things that are unshakable remain. If a thing has been proven to be unshakable by God, guess what that means: Not even the devil can shake it off!

Chapter 12
Men that Prayed Another Level of Prayers

The followings are accounts of men of God that prayed another level of prayers. Please read on and let your soul be stirred to prayer.

John Hyde prayed until the heart shifted from its normal position on the left side to the right side.

John Welch said the day was ill spent if he could not stay eight to ten hours in secret solitude with God.

George Muller said: "I pray hours every day. I live in the spirit of prayers; I pray as I walk, when I lie down, and when I rise up; and the answers always come."

Fenelon cried: "In God's name I beseech you, let your prayer nourish your souls as your meals nourish your bodies."

John Knox cried unto the Lord and said: "Oh God, give me Scotland or I die."

Queen Victoria of Great Britain said: "I don't fear the Bretagne/Britannia that ruleth the earth, but I fear the prayer of John Knox."

Charles Finney prayed and the anointing of the Lord came so mightily upon him that everyone to whom he spoke turned to the Lord.

John Wesley said God does nothing but answer prayers. He prayed and he wrote: "You have nothing to do but to save souls."

D. L. Moody, after praying, and with the anointing upon him said: "The world has yet to see what God can do through one man wholly surrendered to God," then he put one leg on Europe and the other on America and shook both continents for God.

William Branwell wrestled with God for thirty-six hours in a sand pit without a morsel of food.

John Fletcher, an English clergyman and author, stained the walls of his room with the breath of his prayers.

Bishop Ken was so much with God that his soul was said to be God enamored.

Charles Simeon, the English revivalist, devoted four hours to God every morning.

Joseph Alliane, an English clergyman, arose at four o'clock for his business of praying till eight o'clock.

Bishop Andres spent the greatest part of five hours everyday in prayers and devotion.

Martin Luther said: "If I fail to spend two hours each morning in prayers, the devil gets the victory throughout the day. I have so much business, I cannot get on without spending three hours daily in prayers."

David Livingstone lived in prayers and literally died upon his knees in prayers.

In the nineteenth century, there came a restoration under the leadership of **William Seymour** in Los Angeles called the *"Azusa Street Revival."* This one-eyed Black American believer lifted up his eyes unto God and prayed concerning the powerlessness of the church. He asked God to restore power and authority to the church.

In 1906, while travailing in prayer, he received the anointing of the Holy Ghost, and speaking in tongues was restored to the church. Their meetings were held in a ramshackle building, and they prayed until fire came on top of the roof. Fire fighters went and tried to quench the presence of God that had manifested as literal fire.

On several occasions, while seated at the pulpit, all in the church could see the face of **Savonarola** seemingly illuminated with a heavenly glow. Sometimes, he would sit at the pulpit lost in prayers or in a trance for two to five hours at a time. He would lie prostrate on the altar steps in the church for hours weeping and praying about the sins of the age and the sins of the church.

As a result of his prayers, revival broke out in Florence, Italy, and all worldly books, songs and carnivals were forbidden. Huge bonfires were made of worldly books, obscene pictures, masks and wigs. Children marched in processions from house to house singing hymns and calling everyone to repent and empty their homes of every vanity.

James devoted his latter years to praying for the church that when he died, his knees were so calloused that they almost resembled the knee of a camel. So, he was called "camel knee."

Rugged **Martin Luther** was intensely human, yet a man of prayer. He wrote: "I judge that my prayer is more than the evil himself."

Father Nash and **Abel Clary**, the intercessors for Charles Finney, lived and died in prayers.

The world cannot exist without praying men and women. Praying men support the world with prayer for its existence. These men shape their world with prayers. "Lord, raise up Christians who will go on their knees in prayer and then on their toes for the lost!"

Chapter 13
The Presence of God shall Fall Mightily

We are in a time that the church of God has gone worldly and the world has gone "churchly," thereby making it difficult to distinguish between the two. The church of God which Christ said He will build and the gates of hell will never prevail against has now become an entertainment center where people go to have pleasure. The church is no longer afraid of sin because it has lost its fear of the Lord and its passion for His presence.

Today, many ministers of the gospel preach the goodness of the Lord in their lives but have forgotten about the holiness of God in the life of a Christian. Today, Christians are no longer afraid to come to the sanctuary of the Lord with sin in their lives because the church has lost its power and the presence of the Almighty.

If you loose the Almighty, you will have the presence of men. The presence of the Almighty sweeps away sin and brings deep conviction to the heart of a sinner for repentance while the presence of man brings a galore of sin —promoting sin. Rather than coming to the Lord with a broken and a contrite spirit which is the sacrifice to God, we come with our dirty hands lifted up and we open our mouths, saying: "We bring the sacrifice of praise . . ." God is saying, "Get thee behind Me, ye workers of iniquity. I don't need your praise but your holiness unto Me."

Thank God, there is a rising generation that carries irresistible and unpredictable prayers; mighty power and unpredictable intelligence, to bring the great awakening.

Chapter 14
You Have Authority

What is Authority?

It is the right to command and to enforce obedience, the right to act; to delegate right or power; or having the power to govern or command.

God is authority and He does everything authoritatively. He has an authoritative opinion, authoritative influence, authoritative decision or precedence, and authoritative right and power to command. God exercises authority and dictates. You can never dictate until you have authority.

God is an Authoritarian and He is the only One in heaven, on earth, and beneath the waters of the earth, that has universal and sovereign authority — independent, paramount, supreme, potent, excellent, unmitigated and dominant:

"In the beginning God created the heaven and the earth. And the earth was without form, and void; and darkness was upon the face of the deep. And the Spirit of God moved upon the face of the waters. And God said, Let there be light: and there was light" (Genesis 1:1-3).

"And God said, Let there be a firmament in the midst of the waters, and let it divide the waters from the waters. And God made the firmament, and divided the waters which were under the firmament from the waters which were above the firmament: ad it was so" (Genesis 1:6-7).

"And God said, Let the waters under the heave be gathered together unto one place, and let the dry land appear: and it was so" (Genesis 1:9).

"And God said, Let the earth bring forth grass, the herb yielding seed, and the fruit tree yielding fruit after his kind, whose seed is in itself, upon the earth: and it was so" (Genesis 1:11).

"And God said, Let there be lights in the firmament of the heaven to divide the day from the night; and let them be for signs, and for seasons, and for days, and years: And let them be for lights in the firmament of the heaven to give light upon the earth: and it was so" (Genesis 1:14-15).

"And God said, Let the waters bring forth abundantly the moving creature that hath life, and fowl that may fly above the earth in the open firmament of heaven. And God created great whales, and every living creature that moveth, which the waters brought forth abundantly, after their kind, and every winged fowl after his kind: and God saw that it was good." (Genesis 1:20-21).

"And God said, Let the earth bring forth the living creature after his kind, cattle, and creeping thing, and beast of the earth after his kind: and it was so" (Genesis 1:24).

You will realize in all these verses of scripture that, when God was creating the world, He used or exercised authority, i.e., "the Word," by saying, Let there be . . . His words were authoritative; they were impregnated with authority.

Universally, God is highest in the heavens and on earth. Living and non-living and there is none greater than He. He is the end of all heights. He seeks advise from nobody and no one advises Him. When He wanted to swear to Abraham, He looked into the past, present and future, and around Him to see whether there was any authority greater than His authority to swear by but He found none. Therefore, He swore by Himself. God, swearing by Himself denotes authority. In other words, God was saying that, "I swear by My own authority:"

> **"That in blessing I will bless thee, and in multiplying I will multiply thy seed as the stars of the heaven, and as the sand which is upon the sea shore; and thy seed shall possess the gate of his enemies; And in thy seed shall all the nations of the earth be blessed; because thou hast obeyed my voice"** (Genesis 22:17-18).

Jesus was a Man of authority. His preaching, healing, and casting out of demons were all done with authority. Once, when Jesus was preaching, He made a strong authoritative statement:

> **"Ye are of your father the devil, and the lusts of your father ye will do. He was a murderer from the beginning, and abode not in the truth, because there is no truth in him. When he speaketh a lie, he speaketh of his own: for he is a liar, and the father of it. And because I tell you the truth, ye believe me not"** (John 8:44-45).

Jesus healed people from sicknesses and infirmities by the God-given authority upon His life:

"And he stood over her, and rebuked the fever; and it left her; and immediately she arose and ministered unto them" (Luke 4:39).

"And he put forth his hand, and touched him, saying, I will: be thou clean. And immediately the leprosy departed from him" (Luke 5:13).

With His authority, Jesus usually commanded:

A person to be well or the evil spirit to leave — **Luke 4:35;**

The winds and waves to be still — **Luke 8:24;**

The person being healed to do something in faith — **Luke 5:24;**

And sometimes, He was touched by the people and they were healed — **Luke 8:44; Matthew 14:36.**

Jesus said:

" . . . **All power is given unto me in heaven and in earth**" (Matthew 28:18).

On the basis of this authority, He commissioned His followers with the authority to make disciples of "all peoples everywhere," and promised to be with them always:

"**...to the end of the age**" (Matthew 28:19-20).

God had chosen to turn over all heavenly and earthly authority to His Son Jesus Christ in repayment for Jesus' obedience. As He did so:

"**. . . God also highly exalted Him, and gave Him a name which is above every name . . .**" (Philippians 2:9).

One of the first things Jesus did with His authority was to give us the Holy Spirit as He promised in John 16:7. In anticipation of this empowerment on His followers, Jesus told them:

"As the Father sent Me, so I send you" (John 20:21).

When God created man, He gave him dominion, which, in other words, is authority over everything on the earth:

"And God said, Let us make man in our image, after our likeness: and let them have dominion over the fish of the sea, and over the fowl of the air, and over the cattle, and over all the earth, and over every creeping thing that creepeth upon the earth. So God created man in his own image, in the image of God created he him; male and female created he them. And God blessed them, and God said unto them, Be fruitful, and multiply, and replenish the earth, and subdue it: and have dominion over the fish of the sea, and over the fowl of the air, and over every living thing that moveth upon the earth" (Genesis 1:26-28).

So, that was the kind of authority God gave to man until disobedience to God in the Garden of Eden caused man to lose that power to the devil. But when Christ came, died and resurrected on the third day, He:

"Blotted out the handwriting of ordinances that was against us, which was contrary to us, and took it out of the way, nailing it to His cross; And having spoiled principalities and powers, He made a shew of them openly, triumphing over them in it" (Colossians 2:14-15).

Jesus Christ has therefore, restored that authority and power back to us so that we could have the dominion we had at first when God created man:

> **"And the seventy returned again with joy, saying, Lord, even the devils are subject unto us through thy name... Behold, I give unto you power to tread on serpents and scorpions, and over all the power of the enemy: and nothing shall be any means hurt you"** (Luke 10: 17, 19).

You have the authority to pray for protection, life, family, ministry, children, properties, etc. The Psalmist says:

> **"The LORD will not cast off His people . . . the LORD is my defence; and my God is the rock of my refuge"** (Psalm 94: 14, 22).

You can also use that authority to prevent things from happening. We often see things or situations (usually unpleasant) about to happen but by taking authority over them, we can prevent them.

I remember years ago, when I was teaching in a classroom at a junior secondary school, there was a teacher there whom I believed was the reason God sent me to that school. I was to teach him the ways of God, and I did exactly that.

One day, because of unavoidable circumstances, he was not able to make it in to school; so, the proprietress sent a note to him that he was fired. Mind you, this proprietress had so much authority that she usually does not go back on her words. No one could convince her to change her mind or decisions.

However, by the power vested in me, I authorized the man to come to school the following day. I prayed and forbade the devil by the authority given to me in the name of Jesus. He came to school and the proprietress could not utter a word. This teacher taught at the school until he was ready to leave the school.

If you realize that there is a situation in your life that you think (believe) is not the will of God, you can stop it by the authority of Christ. You can boldly declare, *"Satan, you are the cause of this situation, and I forbid you in the name of Jesus. Stop it in Jesus' Name."*

We have the authority to tell the devil to take his hands off our finances, our destiny, our future, and our ministry. We are loaded with authority to attack the devil; we can stop him in his tracks. We can assert our authority by attacking the devil and stopping his works, plans, and activities.

You have so much authority that the devil has to obey whatever you say. In fact, anytime you exercise your authority over the devil, you are commanding him to do your will and desire. You are also enforcing obedience on him.

Our authority has supreme influence over the devil, and his demons. The believer has been given authority to put things right, to make a way for the will of God to prevail, and to thwart the works of the devil.

If you speak with the authority of Jesus Christ, there will be a performance of what you say. For example, if you say, "I am a winner," you will win; "I am an over taker," you will overtake; "I am prosperous," you will prosper because there is authority backing what you say. God's authority is a divine authority by which things are established. Things are enforced by sovereign sanction and empowerment from on high:

"Wherefore neither thought I myself worthy to come unto thee: but say in a word, and my servant shall be healed. For I also am a man set under authority, having under me soldiers, and I say unto one, Go, and he goeth; and to another, Come, and he cometh; and to my servant, Do this, and he doeth it" (Luke 7:7-8).

This is a profound illustration given about power and authority in Hal Lindsey and C.C. Carlson's book **Satan Is Alive And Well On Planet Earth**. You may be wondering what the difference is between power and authority in the life of a Christian.

There is a great deal of difference. In the Greek translation of the New Testament, two words are consistently used for the two concepts. The word "Dunamis" is used to describe the power of the Holy Spirit that operates within the Christian. Unfortunately, the translators are not always consistent in translation the word "Exousia" into the English word "Authority." "Exousia" or "Authority" means delegated power.

Dr. F. Huegel, a great Christian theologian was distinguishing between power and authority to Hal Lindsey while they were sitting near the great boulevard in Mexico City — the Avenue Reforma — and discussing the believer's authority over the demonic world when he narrated this story:

He told of a group of young Mexican boy scouts who were trying to cross the Avenue Reforma during the wild rush-hour traffic. They made it half way across the broad street and took refuge on the esplanade in the center of the street. At the corner of the esplanade, there was a special pedestal where the traffic officer stood to direct traffic. The boys watched as the traffic officer raised his right hand and all the powerful speeding automobiles screeched to a halt.

In Mexico City, that pedestal is a place of authority, and all motorists know it. About this time, a slight accident occurred nearby, and the officer left his place to investigate. While the officer was arguing with the motorists, one of the boys stepped up on the pedestal and raised his right hand. Cars began to grind to a halt instantly. You see, the motorists recognized that the boy was standing in a place of authority. Anyone standing on the pedestal had the full power of the Mexican government backing him or her.

Suppose that boy had physically tried to stop one of those powerful automobiles. That would have been a case of putting his power against the car's power and you can guess who the loser would be.

This is what happens when we try to deal with the devil in our own power. We get steam-rolled! But the motorists had to stop even when a small boy stood in the place of authority because all of the power of the Mexican government was invoked with just the wave of his right hand.

The same principle applies when we realize our place of authority in Christ and step into it. In our case, we have all God's power backing us, and even Satan has to respect that and back off. To assert authority is to operate in the realm of delegated power. The greatness of authority is proportionate to the greatness of the power of the one who delegated it. In the case of the believer's authority, the greatest power in the universe is Jesus Christ, the One to Whom all authority in heaven and earth has been given.

Beloved, it is written in Colossians that Jesus stripped Satan and his demons of their authority. Also, He disarmed those hostile powers so that we may have the victory. In Christ Jesus, we are more than conquerors:

"And having spoiled principalities and powers, he made a shew of them openly, triumphing over them in it" (Colossians 2:15).

Satan is like a toothless bulldog. He can growl and intimidate but he has no authority to back up his threats in the life of a believer. Satan was defeated more than two thousand years ago. Today, he is still defeated. In the future, he will remain defeated. In fact, he is a defeated foe and a vanquished enemy.

I remember when I was going to one of the Embassies in Accra, Ghana to obtain a visa. I asserted my authority in Christ through the Word of God that declares that wherever the soles of my feet shall tread upon, God will give it to me as an inheritance just as He told Abraham. I declared that as the soles of my feet treaded upon the grounds of the embassy and I also decreed that I would not be denied or rejected and that the eyes of the consular officer would be blinded to anything that would disqualify me. I obtained the visa without struggle.

If you know your authority or the power that has been delegated to you by the Authoritarian, you would not walk in defeat but in victory and as a conqueror.

Chapter 15
The Workability of Prayers

When I say "The Workability of Prayers," I mean prayer works. Prayer is an agency of the force of unlimited power. It is also unlimited in creative ability and has virtually unlimited authority or influence over men, nations, churches, and the world.

Prayer is multifarious because it has great diversity. It has the divine potentiality to change the cause of nations, to shape the destiny of men, nations, and churches, to depopulate hell and to populate heaven. Prayer has the power to bless and curse, to kill and to make alive. Prayer is capacitated in bringing men under divine influence of the Almighty God.

For centuries, prayers have stopped the vomits of hell on earth. Over the years, God has used men of prayer to avert the verdicts of satanic predictions and projections and has brought men to the saving knowledge of Christ. That is why, beyond a shadow of doubt, prayer is as vast as God, and prayer can do anything God can do. Prayer has omnipotent power.

If there is anything in this world which is dangerous, which is most terrifying and to be feared, it is a man that prays. The man that prays has omnipotent power residing in him. Whatever he "speaks" is sanctioned by the Omnipotent Power Himself —The Almighty God —and is highly capacitated in coming to pass speedily without an iota of His Word falling to the ground because it has divine backing.

Those who have gone on their knees and prayed made landmarks and, even after their deaths, those landmarks still exist. For people like Jonathan Edwards, John Hyde, John Knox, D. L. Moody and Charles Finney, every landmark required a "knee mark."

"And there were seven sons of one Sceva, a Jew, and chief of the priests, which did so. And the evil spirit answered and said, Jesus I know, and Paul I know; but who are ye? And the man in whom the evil spirit was leaped on them, and overcame them, and prevailed against them, so that they fled out of that house naked and wounded" (Acts 19:14-16).

The man that prays is not a "fearer" of Satan but a "fearer" of God, which means he does not fear Satan, he fears God. The Bible says:

"The fear of the Lord is the beginning of wisdom" (Psalms 111:10).

The man that prays is bold and cannot be intimidated by men. He has the Spirit of the Lord upon him and has favor with both God and man. The man that prays is available to an available God for an available time and mission, and he finishes a God-given mission he starts. If there is any body that God has ever used, it is a man that prays.

The man that prays is never weary even though he is "flesh" and by nature should get weary from time to time. As a result of his prayers, he has the totality, entirety and wholeness of Christ's divine nature so that whatever he does is supernaturally empowered by the Almighty God. Therefore, he never becomes weary:

> **"But they that wait upon the LORD shall renew their strength; they shall mount up with wings as eagles; they shall run, and not be weary; and they shall walk, and not faint"** (Isaiah 40:31).

The man that prays accelerates the purpose of God to cause it to happen ahead of time.

(15.1) The Believer's Armour

The Bible tells all believers to:

> **"Put on the whole Armour of God, that ye may be able to stand against the wiles of the devil"** (Ephesians 6:11).

The Bible says we are not fighting flesh and blood, but unseen beings with personalities and without bodies. The spirits energize our flesh with unnatural cravings:

> **"For we wrestle not against flesh and blood, but against principalities, against powers, against the rulers of the darkness of this world, against spiritual wickedness in high places"** (Ephesians 6:12).

Satan is constantly on guard, watching every believer and waiting for his armour to slip even at the slightest moment so that he can fling his fiery darts:

"Wherefore take unto you the whole armour of God, that ye may be able to withstand in the evil day, and having done all, to stand" (Ephesians 6:13).

Let me help you to understand the different parts of the believer's armour. First we will examine the belt.

(1) **The Belt**

I realize that before Apostle Paul wrote his letter to the Ephesians, he had closely examined the Roman soldiers for months, or maybe years. I also believe that he had a great chance to observe pieces of the soldiers' armour at close range:

"Stand therefore, having your loins girt about with truth, and having on the breastplate of righteousness" (Ephesians 6:14).

The Roman army had the finest armour in the ancient world and Apostle Paul used it as an illustration of the armour God has made available for the Christian to use against Satan. In the Roman soldier's armour, the girdle was the belt and was six to eight inches wide. It was one of the most important pieces of equipment because everything else was fastened to the belt. If the belt was not in place, then the armour would not be secure.

In other words, Apostle Paul was saying that *the believer's basic piece of armour is the truth – the Scriptures.* The believer or the Christian must have a foundation in the Scriptures as well as good knowledge of it. This demands continuous or persistent reading of the Scriptures to become well-vested in the Word of God. The Christian must have an understanding of and know how to apply the Word.

God wants us to have a strong defensive armour against the wiles of Satan. A soldier does not put on his armour after going to battle, but rather in preparation for battle. The belt of truth must be secure or everything else will fall off!

(2) <u>The Breastplate of Righteousness</u>

In the Roman armour, there is a breastplate which was made of bronze baked with tough pieces of hide. It protects one of the most vital areas of the body — the heart.

The breastplate of our armour protects our hearts in righteousness from the attacks of Satan. This refers to the righteousness of Christ:

> **"For he hath made him to be sin for us, who knew no sin; that we might be made the righteousness of God in him"** (2 Corinthians 5:21).

It is only the righteousness of Christ, which clothes us, and that can protect our heart from the missiles of the evil one. God sees us as righteous in Christ.

(3) <u>Boots</u>

> **"And your feet shod with the preparation of the gospel of peace"** (Ephesians 6:15).

In boxing or wrestling which involves hand-to-hand combat, a sure footing is most important because if you lose your footing (or your balance), you will be knocked down or out. When fighting with a sword, as in the time of the Roman legions, losing one's footing could mean death. So, the G.I. issue in footgear at that time was hobnail sandals. When fighting in face-to-face combat, their feet were planted solid so that their footing was sure.

In our Christian life, we need solid footing too, if we are going to walk and resist the devil. *That solid footing is provided by the Gospel of Peace.* There is no peace that comes from anywhere but the gospel. The gospel of peace is absolute, dependable and complete. In fact, the human mind cannot comprehend it.

"And the peace of God, which passeth all understanding, shall keep your hearts and minds through Christ Jesus" (Philippians 4:7).

(4) Shield

"Above all, taking the shield of faith, wherewith ye shall be able to quench all the fiery darts of the wicked" (Ephesians 6:16).

A Roman soldier's shield was about two feet wide and four feet long. He used it to ward off the blows of the enemy and also to hide behind when the enemy archers released a volley of arrows. Sometimes, the Roman soldiers would kneel down on the ground and erect a wall of shields around them to block out the flaming missiles. Satan is

always firing his hot, fiery darts at us. He is always trying
to get inside us with guilt or some form of accusation. If
you have the shield of faith protecting you — *that simple,
implicit faith in the fact that Christ is more than able to meet
your needs* — you have adequate protection right there.

(5) <u>Helmet</u>

"**And take the helmet of salvation …**" (Ephesians 6:17).

The helmet, of course, protects the head — another area
that needs to be guarded from fatal blows. This is a
vital piece in the Roman armour just as it is in ours. **The
helmet of salvation represents the knowledge that your
salvation is absolutely secure and complete.** Once you
believe in Jesus Christ, your sins are forgiven not only
for the present, but also for the past and the future.

Once you believe in Christ, the devil cannot take you
out of the will of God because you are under the covering
of the Almighty:

> "**And I give unto them eternal life; and they shall
> never perish, neither shall any man pluck them out
> of my hand. My Father, which gave them me, is
> greater than all; and no man is able to pluck them
> out of my Father's hand. I and my Father are one**"
> (John 10:28-30).

Satan is a "perverter" of the Word of God. When he tempted
Jesus Christ in the wilderness, Jesus quoted the Scriptures
to him saying:

"It is written . . ." (Luke 4:4, 8).

In the last temptation, however, the devil also quoted the Scriptures to Jesus, saying:

"It is written . . ." (Luke 4:10).

One thing that we must realize is that Satan is not ignorant of the Word of God. Since he knows the Word, he makes every attempt to distort it. That is why as Christians, we need the helmet of salvation. There are many people who are virtually on the brink of mental illness because they think they have lost their salvation. This is because they receive persistent accusations from the devil probably because of some sins they committed. The devil deceives them that their sin is terrible, unpardonable, and beyond forgiveness.

Dearly beloved, once you have given your life to Christ, you have been forgiven. Salvation does not depend on performance. It never has and it never will.

(6) Sword

". . . And the sword of the Spirit, which is the word of God . . ." (Ephesians 6:17).

The Word of God, which is symbolic of the sword, is an offensive weapon. It has a blade that is about twenty-four inches long. It is sharp on both edges and is pointed at the end. The design of this sword was important. A trained Roman legionnaire could thrust and cut from any position so that he was not caught off balance. The opposing soldiers who had larger swords had to get into certain positions to swing at them. The Roman soldier would duck, catch his opponent off balance, and finish him off before he (the opponent) could crawl back for another swing:

> **"For the word of God is quick, and powerful, and sharper than ay two-edged sword. . . ."** (Hebrews 4:12).

We can only defeat the enemy on the battlefield if we are soaked in the Word of God. With the Word of God, the devil cannot knock us off balance by his onslaughts. When Jesus was tempted by the devil, He knew that the only thing that could defeat the devil and cause him to flee was quoting the Scriptures to him (Luke 4). Therefore, the only way we can resist the devil is to stand on God's Word against him. The devil flees from the one who uses the Word against him **(James 4:7):**

(7) <u>Prayer</u>

> **"Praying always with all prayer and supplication in the Spirit, and watching thereunto with all perseverance and supplication for all saints"** (Ephesians 6:18).

The sword of the Spirit and prayers are the Christian's offensive weapons. If there is anything that can keep Satan from counter-attacks, it is the Word of God and prayers.

The Bible says that God is a God that answers prayers, and unto Him shall the gathering of His people be. Beloved, it is not because of your profound and lengthy phrases, but because He is a living God, and He answers prayers.

Summary:

After a study of the armour of God, we need to find out whether we are keeping it polished and oiled at all times — ready for active duty. If our sword is rusty because we have not been studying the Word, we better sharpen it. If our breastplate is slipping out of place because we are getting our performance kicked, we better adjust it. If our helmet is off because we are not sure of our salvation, then we better get into the Word of God or go to someone who knows the Word and make sure it is in place.

We cannot afford to be tin soldiers. We do not dare play games with the devil; he is capturing men right and left — on all sides — and is using all his arsenal to achieve this:

"For we wrestle not against flesh and blood, but against principalities, against powers, against the rulers of the darkness of this world, against spiritual wickedness in high places" (Ephesians 6:12).

Real spiritual beings are becoming bold enough to come out in the open and influence people. These people are willing to worship Satan who is still practicing his subtle ways on them because they chose not to believe that he exists. In fact, the devil is having a field day with them!

As you whistle to the armoury troops, make sure your armour is in place. In this century, the devil is about to experience (and is actually experiencing) a defeat he has never experienced before over the centuries.

(15.2) Divine Groanings

The following will help you to understand what the Bible says about divine groaings.

> **"Lord, all my desire is before thee; and my groaning is not hid from thee"** (Psalm 38:9):

> **"And it came to pass in process of time, that the king of Egypt died: and the children of Israel sighed by reason of the bondage, and they cried, and their cry came up unto God by reason of the bondage. And <u>God heard their groaning</u>, and God remembered his covenant with Abraham, with Isaac, and with Jacob. And God looked upon the children of Israel, and God had respect unto them"** (Exodus 2:23-25).

> **"Now therefore, behold, the cry of the children of Israel is come unto me: and I have also seen the oppression wherewith the Egyptians oppress them"** (Exodus 3:9).

Heaven is not moved by man's oratory, but it will be moved by tears and agony of the soul. There is much that ought to cause agony of the soul these days. For instance, the church's apostasy and ineffectiveness, the world's indifference and wickedness, and the latter because of the former.

The church is the light and salt in a dark and corrupt world. So, if the light is darkness and the salt has lost its savor, what hope is there for a poor and fallen world? It is useless to rail against the world's indifference if our hearts are not moved with compassion over the "shepherd-less" sheep.

The need of the day is for men and women who can groan in prayer. Those who acutely feel the present situation and who are under the burden of the world's need to such an extent that fasting, praying and absenting themselves from social circles until their burden is lifted and deliverance is come, is not a self-inflicted penance.

Christ receives our sighs in His censer for prayers, and even though others mock at our groans, He made us know what they mean. The Spirit also makes us know what they mean. He first makes the signs as an intercessor and then God hears it—He is praying within and without hearing. A beggar gets alms at Christ's gate even by making signs.

The Lord does not regard:

The grammatical structure of prayers—how we word our prayers;

The arithmetic of prayers—how often we pray;

The rhetoric of prayers—how fine we pray; or

The music of prayers—the sweetness of the tone we use in prayers.

The Lord is moved by divine groaning. Francis Raworth once said, *"There are sighs and groans which cannot be uttered."*

A burning Niagara of words does not impress or move God. Hannah, Samuel's mother, one of the most profound intercessors had no language:

> **"And she was in bitterness of soul, and prayed unto the LORD, and wept sore . . .**
>
> **Now Hannah, she spake in her heart; only her lips moved, but her voice was not heard . . ."** (1 Samuel 1:10, 13).

There is groaning that cannot be uttered. In the mountain-moving place of travailing prayers, linguists are not needed. "Hannah spoke in her heart." When the heart is full of grief, it can only groan in prayer. Yet, David the Psalmist says, *". . . My groaning is not hid from Thee."* "Groanings which cannot be uttered" are often prayers which are unavoidable and undeniable by God.

Prayers characterized by groaning is the Christian's greatest resource and the one least used. It is the Christian's greatest obligation and the one most neglected. It is the most common form of devotion, yet the one least understood. Prayer is the gateway to God's presence, but few enter into it. Prayer is the channel of God's grace, which in most lives is clogged.

It is commonly assumed that anyone can pray, but only those who have accepted Christ have full access to God. Many regard groaning prayer as optional, but God requires prayer as the condition for Him to work. Where there is no prayer, there is no omnipotent power.

If a finger can be pointed to the greatest thing lacking among the laity, the ministers, and Christians at large, I would not hesitate to point to the need for an effective prayer life that is characterized by agonizing and groaning. E. M. Bounds once said, *"The Church that is dependent on its history for miracles of power and grace is a fallen church."*

The destitution in the light of eternity is awful; it stares us in the face. Human efforts cannot meet it. Nothing short of the power of divine groaning in prayer can! So groan in prayer.

Ah, where are those who can groan in prayers? The power of prayer is not only the most direct and effective force that can be brought to bear upon the many difficult problems that exist in the Lord's work, but it has the greater advantage of being free from human schemes and carnal manipulations. The whole purpose of a life of prayer is to bring us to the place of crucifixion, and to school us in the great principles of righteousness, justice and love.

Chapter 16
Until Ascension, There Is No Anointing

At this point, I would like to emphasize that in order for there to be an anointing, there must need be an ascension in prayer. Those who are willing to ascend in another level of prayer will descend with a great anointing:

> "And it came to pass, when they were gone over, that Elijah said unto Elisha, Ask what I shall do for thee, before I be taken away from thee. And Elisha said, I pray thee, let a double portion of thy spirit be upon me. And he said, Thou hast asked a hard thing: nevertheless, if thou see me when I am taken from thee, it shall be so unto thee; but if not, it shall not be so" (2 Kings 2:9-10).

Elijah is not the giver of the anointing. God is. Jesus said, *"After I have gone, the Father will send the Holy Spirit in My name."* It is God that sends/gives the anointing, not man. Elijah had no power to bestow a *"double portion"* of his spirit upon his successor, Elisha. All that Elijah could do was to intercede for Elisha that his request would be granted.

Here, Elijah typifies Christ as our intercessor, while Elisha typifies the disciples. As Elijah interceded for Elisha's request to be granted, so also Christ intercedes for us that our prayers to the Father would be answered:

> "And he said, Thou has asked a hard thing: nevertheless, if thou see me when I am taken from thee, it shall be so unto thee; but if not, it shall not be so. And it came to pass, as they still went on,

and talked, that, behold, there appeared a chariot of fire, and horses of fire, and parted them both asunder; and Elijah went up by a whirlwind into heaven" (2 Kings 2:10-11).

"And Elisha saw it, and he cried, My father, my father, the chariot of Israel, and the horsemen thereof. And he saw him no more: and he took hold of his own clothes, and rent them in two pieces" (2 Kings 2:12).

"He took up also the mantle of Elijah that fell from him, and went back, and stood by the bank of Jordan; And he took the mantle of Elijah that fell from him, and smote the waters, and said, Where is the LORD God of Elijah? And when he also had smitten the waters, they parted hither and thither: and Elisha went over. And when the sons of the prophets which were to view at Jericho saw him, they said, The spirit of Elijah doth rest on Elisha. And they came to meet him, and bowed themselves to the ground before him" (2 Kings 2:13-15).

The prayer of Elisha for a double portion of Elijah's spirit is reflected in the prayer of the early Church for the Holy Spirit:

"And I will pray the Father, and he shall give you another Comforter, that he may abide with you for ever; Even the Spirit of truth; whom the world canot receive, because it seeth him not, neither knoweth him: but ye know him; for he dwelleth with you, and shall be in you . . . But the Comforter, which is the Holy Ghost, whom the Father will send in

my name, he shall teach you all things, and bring all things to your remembrance, whatsoever I have said unto you" (John 14:16-17, 26).

Just as Elisha could not receive the double portion until Elijah was caught up to heaven, so the followers of Christ could not receive the Holy Spirit until Jesus ascended to heaven. Jesus said:

"Nevertheless I tell you the truth; It is expedient for you that I go away: for if I go not away, the Comforter will not come unto you; but if I depart, I will send him unto you" (John 16:7).

If the Lord's disciples could believe this, if with the eye of faith they saw Jesus indeed rise from the dead, if they saw Him ascend into heaven and sit at the right hand of the Father, then they could do greater than the mighty works that Jesus did:

"Verily, verily, I say unto you, He that believeth on me, the works that I do shall he do also; and greater works than these shall he do; because I go unto my Father" (John 14:12).

In our petition for the anointing of God's Spirit upon our lives and ministries, we must keep our eyes on Christ at all times; and we must move forward with God. We dare not tarry at Bethel or linger with the sons of the prophets at Jericho. We must die to ourselves. This is typified by Elijah and Elisha's passage through the Jordan, which is symbolic of death. In our spiritual walk, we must fix our eyes on no one else but Christ.

While the gift of the Holy Spirit is upon all believers, receiving a double portion is another matter. This double portion is only meant for people, like Elisha, whose eyes are on Christ alone and who have made prayer their business — their supreme business.

If all believers would pray, make intercession, and ascend in the fervency of agonizing and travailing prayers, there will be a descending of the mighty works that Jesus did; even greater works. If we will ascend in another level of prayers, we will descend storming the gates of hell and destroying the works of the devil. Only those who ascend to another level of prayers can descend dynamiting the strongholds of Satan:

> **"And being in an agony he prayed more earnestly: and his sweat was as it were great drops of blood falling down to the ground"** (Luke 22:44).

Many believe the truth of Jesus' victory over Satan on the cross, but before that, Jesus had the upper hand over Satan in the garden of Gethsemane. It was there He prayed and ascended in the spirit of prayer and descended having victory over His enemy before going to the Cross. His crucifixion was the manifestation of the victory He already had over Satan in the garden of Gethsemane:

> **"Blotting out the handwriting of ordinances that was against us, which was contrary to us, and took it out of the way, nailing it to his cross; And having spoiled principalities and powers, he made a shew of them openly, triumphing over them in it"** (Colossians 2:14-15).

Chapter 17
Warfare Evangelism

I remember when I was in the eleventh grade, the Lord gave me a revelation one Saturday afternoon. I was relaxing on my bed and was half asleep in what I would call "a trance" when, suddenly, I saw numerous people walking on a very broad road. An audible and peaceful voice from the clouds asked me, "Do you know these people walking on this road?" I answered, "no," and the voice told me that all the people I just saw were doomed and were going to hell.

I woke up from my bed panicking after considering the number of people who were bound for hell, and then the Holy Spirit started ministering to me. He asked me to get a notepad and write down what I had seen and what He was about to tell me. He ministered many things to me that afternoon, most of which I am unable to share in this book.

He told me that most of His "ministers" have failed Him. These ministers are seeking fame, wealth, and prominence and are competing with one another. They have forgotten about the "Great Commission" which is the supreme and primary task of the church of Jesus Christ.

After hearing these things, I could not contain the heaviness in my spirit. So, I began to intercede for the perishing souls, pastors, prophets, evangelists, teachers, and apostles who have relegated to the background the purpose of their calling and were pursuing their own agenda. My prayer was for God to forgive them and make them return to their senses. This was when my passion for perishing souls and intercessory prayers was birthed:

"And he saith unto them, Follow me, and I will make you fishers of men" (Matthew 4:19).

As I mentioned in an earlier chapter, according to the United States Center For World Mission, there are still 2.5 billion people in the world that live in more than 16,000 ethnic groups or tribes. An ethnic group is a group of people that has its own culture, language, tradition, etc. These 16,000 groups or 2.5 billion people have never heard the Gospel of Jesus Christ.

Kenya, which has thousands of preachers, is a few hours from Somalia and many surrounding tribes that have never been reached with the gospel. There are also hundreds of missionaries in Kenya, and there are between two hundred and two hundred and fifty Pentecostal churches in Nairobi alone. Still, there are more than 40 tribes in Kenya that have not yet heard the Gospel of Jesus Christ. There are 14,000 villages in Ghana that have no Christian witness. The Book of Revelation says:

"Saying, I am Alpha and Omega, the first and the last: and, What thou seest write in a book, and send it unto the seven churches which are in Asia; unto Ephesus, and unto Smyrna, and unto Pergamos, and unto Thyatira, and unto Sardis, and unto Philadelphia, and unto Laodicea" (Revelation 1:11).

The churches mentioned in the above scripture can be located in the present day Turkey which is half European and half Asian. Yet, 99.7% of the population are Moslem. There are no churches in countries like Saudi Arabia, Dakar, Kuwait, the United Arab Emirates and North Yemen.

North Yemen has a population of 100% Moslems

Somalia's population is 99.8% Moslem

Cosmos Islands' population is 99.7% Moslem

Mauritania's population is 99.6% Moslem

Morocco's population is 99.6% Moslem

Algeria's population is 99.5% Moslem

Tunisia's population is 99.5% Moslem

Afghanistan's population is 99.0% Moslem, and

Iran's population is 99.8% Moslem.

In some Western European countries, the church is losing ground. Thousands of churches are being closed in Russia. In the real estate business in England, 800 to 1000 church buildings are listed for sale. The churches were closed because attendance had fallen drastically. In Holland and many European countries, Moslems buy these large church buildings and turn them into mosques, restaurants and casinos. There are six hundred million people on the African continent, but only 14% are Christians:

> **"The Lord is not slack concerning his promise, as some men count slackness; but is longsuffering to us-ward, not willing that any should perish, but that all should come to repentance"** (2 Peter 3:9).

The supreme task of the church is world evangelization. When God loved, He loved a world. When He gave His Son, He gave Him for a world. When Christ died, He died for a world. God's vision is a world vision, and that is the vision He wants us to have. So, let us arise and take this world for Christ.

When we talk of world evangelism or evangelizing a country or nation, it is often thought that the answer is in strategies, technologies, and other "-ologies," conferences and research. While some of these may be needed, it is certain that dry bones will live only when the Holy Spirit gives life:

"Then said he unto me, Prophesy unto the wind, prophesy, son of man, and say to the wind, Thus saith the Lord GOD; Come from the four winds, O breath, and breathe upon these slain, that they may live" (Ezekiel 37:9).

The "Christlessness" in our land are the dry bones. There are two hundred and thirty-five geographical entities, which include countries. Out of these entities, ninety-seven are closed to the Gospel of Jesus Christ. It is estimated that three billion people live in these ninety-seven nations that are closed to the gospel.

In the midst of all this, how much does the church earnestly implore God to empower them? We organize conferences and strategize, but how much emphasis is placed on waiting on God to descend in our revivals? In spite of all the technological and communication advancements, we still need God in our midst. We really need the Lord to move; we need the touch of the "Master's Hand." Could it be that our research and strategies have become our new "Baal?" Is the church growing by the invocation of the Holy Spirit? (Acts 9:31).

Ministers, preachers, teachers and Christian are fishing for fame instead of men. We have so much passion — not just passion, but consumable passion for academic excellence, ecclesiastical honors, and theological degrees, yet we have moved far away from the simple commission of the humble Savior:

"O Lord, break our pride and desire for achievements. Remove, O Lord, our desire for human acclaim. Lord, our countries are

burning, but we are playing our theological, mythological and many other illogical fiddles."

This is the time for the church — the body of Christ to break away from technological strangulations and begin to pray and war on our knees for the souls that have not yet been reached with the gospel. This is the time to enter into our closets and bind the activities of the prince of Islam which has held millions of people captive under his deception and is taking them to hell. Now is the time for the Church to rise up and depopulate hell and populate heaven through prayers.

This is a crucial hour. We must arise in the unlimited power of Jehovah in our prayer rooms and churches and terminate the "terminator" of perishing souls. We must halt the power of unbelief and worldliness, and lay hold of, and claim the lost souls which are precious and more important to Him than our nicely decorated messages that have no divine power.

We have stopped preaching about our Savior. We now only preach about ourselves and our accomplishments. As a result, there is no power in our services and we have lost our passion for lost souls. We compete with each other and have become the laughing stock of hell and spiritual nonentities:

"Deliver us, O Lord! We need You in our church services.

We need You in the pastors' prayer closets.

We need Your holy presence at our family alter.

We need You when our Sunday School teachers teach our children.

Father, send down fire from heaven on the true altar and put shame to the altar of any new Baal of godless evangelism.

O Father, visit us. Breathe Your Spirit into us. Descend and dwell among the humble and revive them.

Come, Jehovah Shamah!"

We need to have a burning desire in our hearts once again:

"Come, Lord, we need You! Anoint the pews and pulpit.

Restore, O Lord, the first century Christianity.

Lord, as we go back to the primary purpose of our calling, help us win the world into the fold of Jesus Christ."

"The greatest need of every mission is the manifestation of the Holy Spirit." Where are those amongst us who will cause rivers of living waters to flow?

For the last fifty years, it has been recorded that Christianity has grown by 47% while Buddhism is said to have grown by 63%. Hinduism has grown by 117% during the same period. In some countries today, it is virtually impossible to engage in open evangelism because of religious restrictions.

With situations like these, we do not need methods and strategies even though there may be those who believe that more powerful methods will produce greater results. We need divine power.

We need to rise up in intercession, bombard the geographical gates of hell, and on our knees and in our closets totally annihilate the calculations and schemes of Satan over God's precious souls. The only way to win souls is to become vessels filled with the Holy Spirit. The value of one soul is much more precious to God than the cattle on a thousand hills.

CHAPTER 18
Warriors And Fearless Fighters

"And of the Gadites there separated themselves unto David into the hold to the wilderness men of might, and men of war fit for the battle, that could handle shield and buckler, whose faces were like the faces of lions, and were as swift as the roes upon the mountains" (1 Chronicles 12:8).

The warriors and fearless fighters are like the Gadites men — they are wilderness men of might. Remember that it is only the "wilderness men" that enter the Promised Land. When God delivered the children of Israel from Egypt into the Promised Land, the original generation that was delivered by the mighty hand of Jehovah did not make it to the Promised Land. It was those who were born in the wilderness that made it to the Promised Land.

These wilderness men are also men of war, fit for battle. If our earthly army recruits men who are physically fit and without any deformity, how much more our heavenly Father who is a God of war. He will recruit "able bodies" spiritual and physical men who are spiritually infused and injected with divine boldness and capabilities to apprehend the strategies of the devil. These men can also handle a shield and a buckler. Their faces are like the face of lions and they are as swift as the roses upon the mountains.

According to the scriptures, Jesus Christ is the Lion of the tribe of Judah. This means that these men have the likeness of Christ and are in conformity with His image. These are the people who have been overshadowed by the image and glory of Christ. You can never be part of this army if you do not have the resemblance of Christ. You can never be a good soldier if you do not know how to handle a gun. These warriors are competent men, capable of handling Scriptures and more able to appropriate the blood and the name of Jesus Christ in spiritual warfare:

"And Abishai the brother of Joab, he was chief of the three: for lifting up his spear against three hundred, he slew them, and had a name among the three" (1 Chronicles 11:20).

This end time army is made up of warriors and fearless fighters like Benaiah:

"Benaiah the son of Jehoiada, the son of a valiant man of Kabzeel, who had done many acts; he slew two lionlike men of Moab: also he went down and slew a lion in a pit in a snowy day" (1 Chronicles 11:22).

One very important thing about these warriors and fighters is that they know that it is *"not by their might or power, but it is by the Spirit of the Lord."* They, therefore, go to battle in the name of the Lord knowing not to trust in the arm of the flesh. They also know that *"the name of the Lord is a strong tower, the righteous run into it and are safe."*

David, the man after God's heart, knew a secret which Saul and his three older brothers — Eliab, Abinadab, and Shammah — did not know: The secret of trusting and having faith in the name of the Lord. With this knowledge, David was able to say to Goliath face to face:

"Thou comest to me with a sword, and with a spear, and with a shield: but I come to thee in the name of the LORD of hosts, the God of the armies of Israel, whom thou has defied . . . And all this assembly shall know that the LORD saveth not with sword and spear: for the battle is the LORD's, and he will give you into our hands" (1 Samuel 17:45, 47).

The Bible also records in 1 Chronicles:

"Of Zebulun, such as went forth to battle, expert in war, with all instruments of war, fifty thousand, which could keep rank: they were not of double heart" (1 Chronicles 12:33).

These were specialized warriors who were experts and strategists of war. They only take instructions from their commander-in-chief, Jesus Christ. This explains why "they were not of double heart."

Chapter 19
Travail Brings Birth

"My little children, of whom I travail in birth again until Christ be formed in you . . ." (Galatians 4:19).

"Remember, brethren, our labor and travail: for laboring night and day, because we would not be chargeable unto any of you, we preached unto you the gospel of God" (1 Thessalonians 2:9).

The birth of a child is pre-dated by months of burden and days of travail. So is the birth of a spiritual child. Jesus prayed for His church, but, to bring it to spiritual birth, He gave Himself up unto death. Apostle Paul prayed "night and day . . . exceedingly" for the church. Moreover, he travailed for the sinner. It was when "Zion travailed" that she brought forth.

If the physical birth rate had been as low as the spiritual birth rate has been over the past years and centuries, the human race by now would almost be extinct.

Asking includes making our requests for the salvation of loved ones, but prayer is more than asking. Prayer entails us getting into subjection of the Holy Ghost so that He can work in and through us. In the first chapter of Genesis, everything that had life brought forth its own kind. In regeneration, should not every born again soul bring others to birth?

Women of the Bible who had been barren brought forth their noblest children:

Sarah, who was barren until she was ninety years of age, begat Isaac.

Rachel's cutting cry, "Give me children, or else I die!" was answered and she bore Joseph who delivered the children of Israel.

Manaoh's wife gave birth to Samson, another deliverer of the nation of Israel.

Hannah, a smitten soul, after sobbing in the sanctuary, making vows to God and continuing in prayer, ignored Eli's scorn and poured out her soul to God. She received her answer in the miracle of Samuel who became the prophet of Israel.

Ruth who was a widow also found mercy before God and she gave birth to Obed who gave birth to Jesse. Jesse was the father of King David (the most beloved King of Israel) from whose lineage came our Savior Jesus Christ.

And from Elizabeth who was barren and stricken in years, came John the Baptist, of whom Jesus said there was no greater prophet born of a woman.

What mighty men would have been lost if there were no travails of birth?

It is true that science has alleviated some of the sufferings that our mothers go through in childbirth, but science can never shrink the long and slow months of child formation. In the same way, preachers have methods of bringing souls to the altar, but it is the groaning at the altar that will establish these souls in the house of God.

Leonard Ravenhill once said, *"True revival and soul-birth still demands travail."*

God's greatest gifts to man comes through travail. When we look into the spiritual or temporal (physical) sphere, can we discover any great reform, any beneficial discovery, or any soul-awakening revival which did not come through the toils and tears, the vigil and blood-shedding of men and women whose sufferings were the pangs of its birth?

There is a direct and distinct connection between importunate agonizing and true success, just as there is a connection between travail and birth; the sowing in tears and reaping in joy.

"How is it that your seeds spring up so quickly?" said one gardener to another. *"It is because I sleep with it,"* was the reply. We must all sleep with our teaching in tears *"when none but God is nigh,"* and the growth will surprise and delight us. *"Prayer and pains, with faith in God, can accomplish anything,"* said John Elliot. The person who talks to God has the ability to talk to men without making a mistake.

Bibliography

Bounds, E. M. *Prayer and Praying Men* USA Moody Press,1980.

Leonard, Ravenhill. USA, *Why Revival Tarries,* UK. Bethany House, 1987.

Lindsey, Hal and Carlson, C.C.'s *Satan is Alive and Well on Planet Earth.* USA. Harpercollins, 1992.

Osborn, T. L. *The Purpose of Pentecost.* USA. Osborn Foundation International, 1964.

United States Center for World Missions, USA.

Wesley, Duewel. *Touch the World Through Prayer,* USA. Zondervan Publishing House, 1991.

TO HIS GLORY PUBLISHING COMPANY, INC.

463 Dogwood Dr. Lilburn, GA. 30047, U.S.A (770)458-7947

Order Form for Bookstores in the USA

Order Date: _____

Order Placed By: _____ By Fax: _____

Address: _____

_____

City _____ ST/ZIP _____

Phone #: _____

Email: _____

Purchase Order#: _____

Return Policy: Within 1 year but not before 90 Days.

Price	**Quantity**	**List Price**
Shipping Method:		
Media:		
UPS:		
FedEx:		
Other (Please Secify):		
Total Price:	**Total Quantity:**	**List Price**

Ship To Address: **Bill to Address:**

To His Glory Publishing

Let Us Publish Your Book

To His Glory Publishing Company will publish your book at the least expensive cost. We pay one of the highest royalties in the industry – 40%! We print on demand and place your book on the major online bookstores such a Amazon.com, Barnesandnoble.com, Bookamillion.com, etc.